UNDERSTANDING
FITNESS AND
TRAINING

Ward Lock Riding School

UNDERSTANDING FITNESS AND TRAINING

DAVID HAMER

WARD LOCK

RIDING SCHOOL

WARD LOCK

A WARD LOCK BOOK

First published in the UK 1993
by Ward Lock
A Cassell Imprint
Villiers House
41/47 Strand
LONDON
WC2N 5JE

Distributed in the United States
by Sterling Publishing Co., Inc.
387 Park Avenue South, New York, NY 10016-8810

Distributed in Australia
by Capricorn Link (Australia) Pty Ltd
P.O. Box 665, Lane Cove, NSW 2066

**A British Library Cataloguing in Publication Data block for
this book may be obtained from the British Library**

ISBN 0 7063 7124 0

Typeset by Litho Link Ltd, Welshpool, Powys, Wales

Printed and bound in Great Britain by Hillmans (Frome) Ltd

All photographs by Equestrian Services Thorney

Frontispiece: **Gridwork must be progressive.**

CONTENTS

THE AUTHOR

DAVID HAMER has been working in the horse industry since leaving school both as a stable manager and instructor. He is currently Head of Horse Management at Moulton College in Northampton, where he prepares horses and riders for competitions and examinations. He is a qualified British Horse Society Instructor (BHSI) and Examiner.

INTRODUCTION

Riding is one of today's fastest growing sports. Now competition riders have a choice of a wide range of shows and events in which to participate. Some people compete just for fun, whereas for others the object is to win. Whatever your ambition, it is certainly more pleasurable to ride a fit and correctly trained horse. This book covers many aspects of training and fitness, starting with the selection of the right horse for you.

Correct conformation will enable the horse to perform what is asked of it more easily but a good temperament is also very important. It is therefore very important that the rider or prospective buyer looks at the animal as a whole. When training the horse its physiology and anatomy will affect the way you ride and the fitness programme you choose; its psychology will affect the way the horse reacts to this. Trying to force a horse to perform before its body and mind are prepared will only bring failure and, at worst, result in the horse being injured or rendered useless.

Early training is particularly important in developing discipline and trust and out of this confidence will also grow. The horse will have the confidence to co-operate with its rider and the rider will have

confidence in asking the horse to perform. From this early training, the horse will be able to branch out into the various equestrian disciplines. Whatever type of competitive work it does, the horse must be agile and athletic. This requires basic schooling until the horse is obedient to the aids. The athletic ability of the horse can be enhanced by a combination of dressage and jumping, the one complementing the other.

The successful event horse requires all these qualities, plus the stamina and confidence to tackle a cross country course. Eventing is one of the high-risk disciplines but many accidents can be avoided through correct and careful training.

Although this book concentrates on the training and fitness of horses, it is important to remember that the key to success does largely depend on good stable management. A healthy horse will be able to cope far better with the rigours of training. Good stable management encompasses feeding, stable care and a carefully planned conditioning programme that prepares the horse for its fitness training. Meticulous attention to detail is required in both the care and the training of the horse. This should ensure that you and your equine friend have many happy years together.

CHAPTER 1

CONFORMATION

Perfection is seldom found in this
world and there is even a certain
amount of conjecture as to whether a
horse with perfect conformation
would prove suitable for all types of
work. However, there are certain
basic requirements that are uniform.
These give the horse strength,
soundness and ease of movement and
are best understood by studying its
basic anatomy.

THE SKELETAL FRAME

The basic function of the skeleton is
to form a rigid framework that
supports all the soft parts of the body
and maintains body shape. It protects
certain delicate organs, such as the
brain inside the skull and the spinal
cord in the back bone. The bones
act as attachments for the muscles.
When the muscles pull on these bone
levers, they produce movement. This
point is of great importance when
considering the horse's conformation
because the correct length, angle and
alignment of the bones are necessary
to enable the horse to move well.

JOINTS

Joints occur wherever two or more
bones touch. The system of joints and
muscle attachments allows the free
movement of the skeleton. Joints are

bound together by strong fibrous
tissues called ligaments. The joint
itself is surrounded by a membrane
that produces a lubricating fluid
called synovia. Along with the
cartilage that covers the end of the
bones, the synovia helps to absorb
concussion as well as allowing the
joint to move easily. The joints of the
limbs are particularly susceptible to
damage if the bone alignment is
incorrect. The limb joints should be
large and well defined; any puffiness
or rounding of the joints shows wear
and weakness.

MUSCLES

There are three types of muscles:
1. *involuntary muscles* carry out
bodily functions such as digestion;
2. *cardiac muscle* forms the heart;
3. *voluntary* or *skeletal muscle* moves
the body.
   Skeletal muscles work in
antagonistic (opposite) pairs, which
means that when one muscle
contracts, its pair relaxes.
   The muscles are attached to the
bones by strong cord-like tissues
called tendons. These can be
damaged if they are strained and this
can be quite a problem in the horse's
forelimbs. Skeletal muscles either
bend a joint (flexors) or straighten a
joint (extensors). It is this

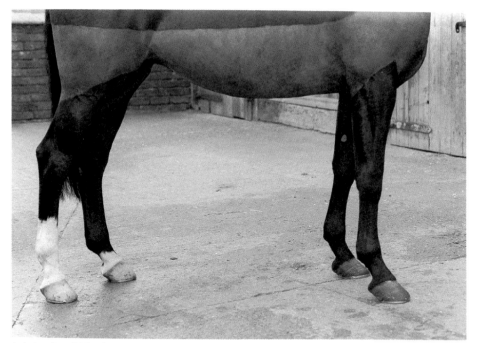

Joints should be large and well defined.

combination of flexion and extension
of joints and the pulling of the bone
levers that creates movement.

The combination of 'make and
shape' of the skeleton and muscles
gives us the horse's conformation.
Good conformation should give an
over-all impression of everything
being in proportion. The main points
of the horse: the poll, withers, croup,
buttock, hock and shoulder should be
well defined. The horse's stifles and
elbows should be in line. This will
give the impression that the horse's
weight is evenly spread over each
limb and therefore the horse will look
well balanced, although it should be
remembered that even well-
proportioned horses will naturally
carry a little more weight on their
forelegs because of the weight of the
head, neck and shoulders.

THE LIMBS

People have different priorities when
assessing a horse's conformation. For
the purpose of good performance, the
limbs and feet should be the first
priority as defects here will render the
horse unsound very quickly. Apart
from this, over-long limbs and
cylindrical feet are not a good design
feature in a horse.

'A leg at each corner' can best
describe what we should look for in
good limbs. The legs should look as if
they support the horse's weight
evenly down to the ground.

The foreleg
The foreleg cannot be discussed
without first considering the
shoulder. The slope of the shoulder
blade (scapula), which is ideally 45

The skeleton.

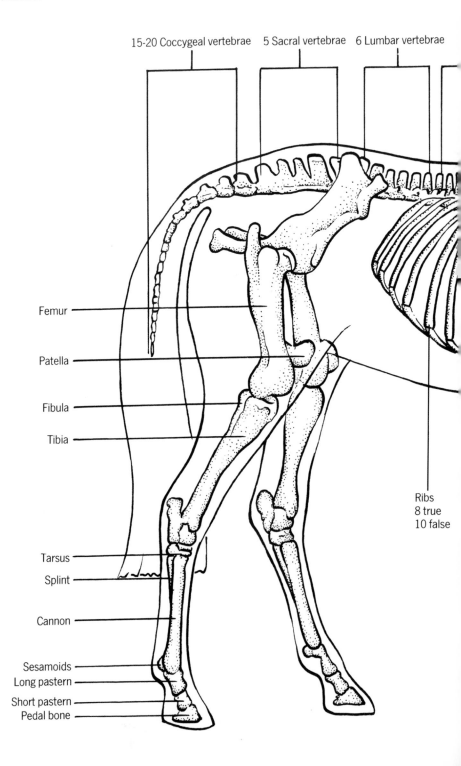

15-20 Coccygeal vertebrae 5 Sacral vertebrae 6 Lumbar vertebrae

Femur

Patella

Fibula

Tibia

Ribs
8 true
10 false

Tarsus

Splint

Cannon

Sesamoids
Long pastern
Short pastern
Pedal bone

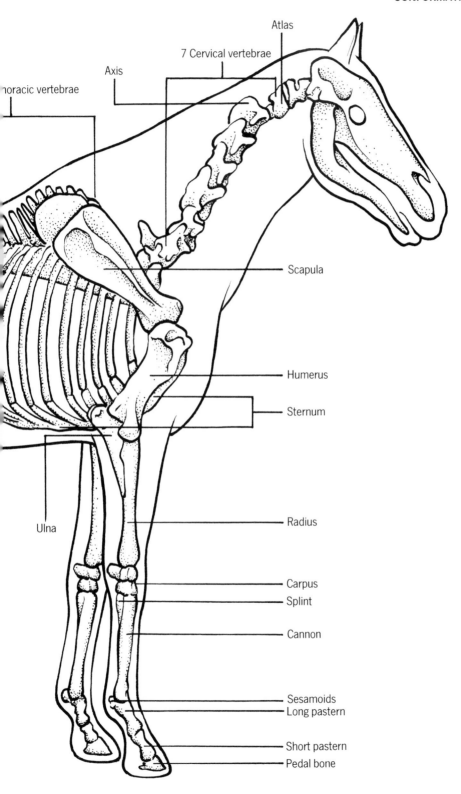

Atlas

7 Cervical vertebrae

Axis

horacic vertebrae

Scapula

Humerus

Sternum

Radius

Ulna

Carpus

Splint

Cannon

Sesamoids

Long pastern

Short pastern

Pedal bone

The superficial muscles.

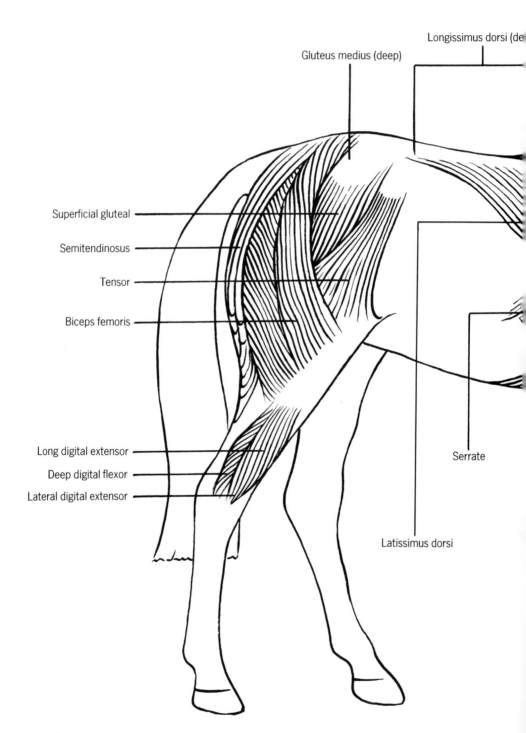

Gluteus medius (deep)

Longissimus dorsi (de

Superficial gluteal

Semitendinosus

Tensor

Biceps femoris

Long digital extensor

Deep digital flexor

Lateral digital extensor

Serrate

Latissimus dorsi

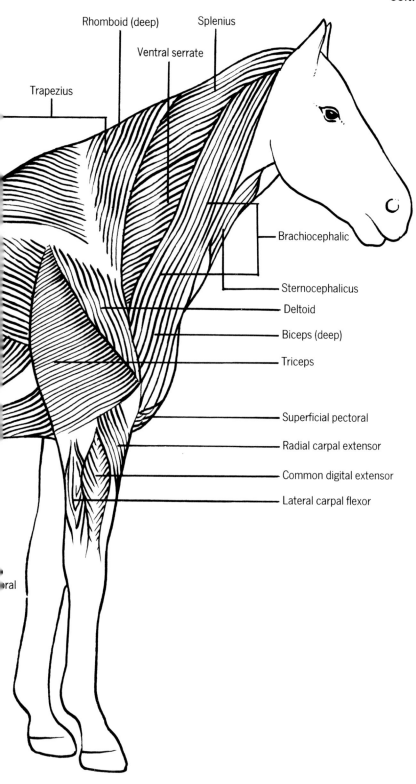

Trapezius

Rhomboid (deep)

Ventral serrate

Splenius

Brachiocephalic

Sternocephalicus

Deltoid

Biceps (deep)

Triceps

Superficial pectoral

Radial carpal extensor

Common digital extensor

Lateral carpal flexor

ral

degrees, and length of the humerus will help to determine the length and comfort (to the rider) of the horse's stride. An upright shoulder, often associated with upright pasterns, will give a short, choppy stride, whereas a long, sloping shoulder will give a free and comfortable stride.

Looking at the forelegs, it should be possible to draw an imaginary vertical line, side on, from the withers through the shoulder and down the middle of the leg. Projection of the knee in front of this line (*over at the knee*) is not desirable, but is far better than the knee coming behind the line (*back at the knee*) as this places strain on the tendons. Looking at the horse from the front, the line should run straight from the point of the shoulder through the middle of the knee to the middle of the toe. Any deviation from this is a weakness and will result in faulty action.

The length of the radius (forearm) in relation to the third metacarpal bone (cannon bone) is important. A long, well-muscled forearm and good sloping shoulder will enable a long, powerful stride, and a short cannon bone will lessen the risk of straining the somewhat vulnerable flexor tendons that run behind it.

The knees should be big, flat and well defined as they will absorb much of the concussion in the foreleg.

The hind leg

The hind leg should be set on so that an imaginary line can be drawn from the point of the buttock, passing down behind the hock and fetlock to the ground. The tibia (second thigh) should be long and well muscled and

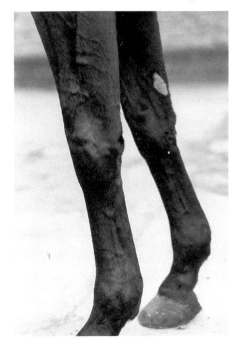

Over at the knee.

Back at the knee.

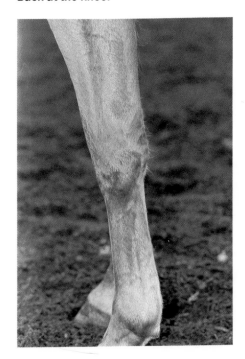

the hock should look as if it is set on low to the ground. The hock itself plays a key role in the action of the hind limb and absorbs a fair amount of concussion, so it should be large in proportion to the horse. The propelling muscles of the hind quarters are the most powerful in the whole body, so good hind leg conformation is very important.

Correct conformation of the hind quarters.

A Good length from the point of hip to the point of buttock for power.
B Good length from point of hip to the point of hock for speed.
C Hind leg set on so that it supports the weight of the hind quarters evenly.

THE FEET

The saying 'No foot, no horse' could not be more true. Many people believe that you should assess a horse's conformation starting from the ground because if the feet are poor then the rest of the conformation is irrelevant. The feet must be matching pairs and give the

impression that they are the right size for the horse. Small boxy feet are often tough, but the horse may well suffer from unsoundness in later life. Flat, shallow feet will bruise easily and the lack of support to the bones in the foot, particularly the small navicular bone at the back of the foot, will lead to unsoundness.

The angle and alignment of the pastern and coffin bones (first, second and third phalanx) are important. These short bones are subjected to a lot of concussion, so the axis of the hoof and the pastern must be equal. From the front, side and back, the horse should appear to spread its weight evenly over the hoof on to the ground.

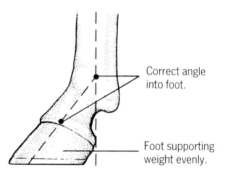

Correct angle into foot.

Foot supporting weight evenly.

Correct hoof/pastern axis.

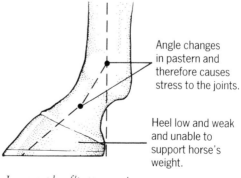

Angle changes in pastern and therefore causes stress to the joints.

Heel low and weak and unable to support horse's weight.

Incorrect hoof/pastern axis.

15

THE HEAD AND NECK

The expression on the horse's face and the way its head and neck are set on will give you a useful first impression. A horse with a 'good outlook' will often gain extra marks in the show or dressage arena.

'A head like a duchess and a bottom like a cook' is supposed to describe a well-made horse. On the other hand, it is also said that beauty is in the eye of the beholder. However, the head should be in proportion to the size of the horse as a big, heavy head will often require a short, strong neck to carry it. The head should be set on so that the poll is its highest point and there should be at least two fingers' width between the jaw bone (mandible) and the

atlas (first cervicle vertebra) to allow for flexion. There should also be at least a fist's width between the jaw bones by the throat, to allow room for the wind pipe and gullet.

The neck should give the appearance of growing from the withers and shoulders to form a natural arc. The muscles over the top of the withers help to lift and move the shoulders, so any dropping away in front of the withers is a weakness. In extreme cases, the neck can even give the appearance of being set on upside down (*ewe necked*). This is a very bad conformation fault and will make it impossible to work the horse correctly.

The length of neck will determine the length of stride, as most of the muscles in the neck are involved in

A ewe neck.

A thick neck.

some way in moving the shoulder and foreleg. This makes it physically impossible for the horse to place its foreleg on the ground in front of its nose when moving.

THE BACK

Again, this must be in proportion to the rest of the horse. A short back is strong and a long back is weak. Short-backed horses can be difficult to sit on in sitting trot and when jumping, whereas long-backed horses are often very comfortable. Mares tend to have slightly longer backs due to the extra space required for the reproductive organs and womb. A good guide is if you can fit a hand's width between the last rib and the point of the hip. When considering the back from the point of view of weakness, you should look at the length of the loins. Strong loins are short and flat across the spine; long loins that slope away from the spine are weak.

Following along the top line to the croup, you should look at the angle of slope and length from the croup to the point of the buttock. A flat croup will often aid speed, where as a sloping croup will make engagement of the hind quarters easier. If the length from the croup to the buttock is short, whether sloping or not it will be weak.

THE CHEST AND GIRTH

The chest should be wide enough to allow the legs to move freely without knocking each other. However, if the chest is too wide, the horse will tend to roll in its gaits. The horse has no collar bone and the chest is slung between the shoulder blades on the strong pectoral muscles and ligaments. The amount of width and room in the chest and girth will give an indication of the amount of room there is for the heart and lungs. In fast work, a big heart and lungs will give the horse an edge.

ACTION AND TYPE

Having studied the principle of good conformation, it becomes apparent that even slight defects in the way a horse is put together can have a considerable effect on the way that it performs and moves. It is also interesting to note that different breeds tend to have different characteristics, which means that their particular conformation makes them more suitable for certain types of work.

Basically, we can classify the horse in two categories: Thoroughbred and non-Thoroughbred.

Thoroughbred

The Thoroughbred has evolved through centuries of careful breeding and has been developed to enable it to race at speed, over either short or long distances. This has resulted in the modern Thoroughbred, a light-framed horse with dense, quality bone. It has a predominance of long, flat muscles that lend themselves to speed. It can have a tendency to be flat in the croup, which results in the hock working a little out behind the horse. This is desirable in the speed horse, but not in the dressage or show jumping horse, so careful selection is important. The Thoroughbred's inherent speed and stamina often

make it suitable for eventing. Some success has also been achieved in dressage, although the Thoroughbred's less-extravagant stride can mean that it is not marked as high as other breeds in international competitions. Its sensitive temperament requires a patient and consistent rider.

Non-Thoroughbreds

Many breeds fall into this category, including the British native breeds, the Arab and many European and American breeds. By crossing these breeds with the Thoroughbred, some useful and quality animals have been produced. In cross-breeding non-Thoroughbred characteristics have often been used to correct and complement Thoroughbred qualities. One example of this is the popular Welsh cob/Thoroughbred cross. The cob gives the rounder action favoured for dressage, while the Thoroughbred gives lightness and quality.

The Arab is renowed for its stamina, but its tendency to be rather high and flat in its croup makes it less suitable for dressage or jumping. The warm blood has become very popular, particularly for dressage and show jumping, because of its round and powerful action.

The careful selection and grading of these horses for breeding, based on their conformation and ability, has resulted in high quality horses. Careful breeding programmes have been lacking in Britain in the past but this situation is now improving. It is interesting to note that the modern warm blood has had a considerable amount of Thoroughbred introduced into its breeding lines.

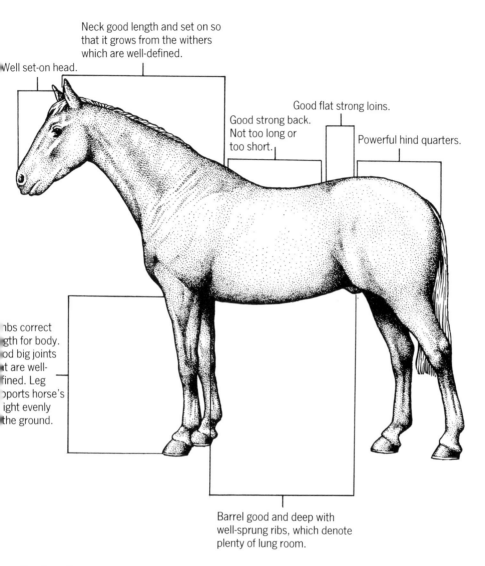

Neck good length and set on so that it grows from the withers which are well-defined.

Well set-on head.

Good flat strong loins.

Good strong back. Not too long or too short.

Powerful hind quarters.

nbs correct
gth for body.
od big joints
it are well-
fined. Leg
pports horse's
ight evenly
the ground.

Barrel good and deep with well-sprung ribs, which denote plenty of lung room.

Good conformation.

SELECTING THE RIGHT HORSE

In brief, good conformation is essential. For work that requires speed and stamina, a horse that is at least three-quarters Thoroughbred is ideal. Having said this, however, after good conformation must come good temperament. Even the most brilliant horse is not going to achieve much if it does not have the right mental attitude to the work. Lastly, the action should be as good as possible. The freer and straighter the horse moves, the less likely it is to damage itself and the easier it will find its work.

Choosing the right breed for you

Thoroughbred
Pros   Fast with lots of spirit
Intelligent and responsive
to training
Excellent cross
Cons May be temperamental or
neurotic
Sensitive and less robust
than other breeds
Less extravagant paces than
other breeds

Arab
Pros   Lots of stamina
Intelligent with presence
and spirit
Speed
Useful cross
Cons Can be neurotic and wilful
Does not always jump well
Sometimes has a high head
carriage which can spoil a
dressage test

Warm blood
Pros   Good temperament
Jumping ability
Good paces
Excellent cross with TB
Cons Lacks speed of TB

Pony breeds
Pros   Good temperament
Intelligence
Stamina
Nimble and sure footed
Good cross with faster,
larger breeds
Cons Lack of speed
Small stature
Can be wilful and stubborn

The more temperamental breeds need to be kept interested in their work. They require variety and a sufficient amount of work to prevent boredom which can lead to stable vices such as box walking, weaving, etc. They can be difficult to keep in good condition as stress may cause them to stop eating or fret weight off. It is a good idea to turn such horses out for part of every day to promote mental relaxation. They need to be well rugged up in the winter.

The less temperamental breeds may tend to become fat very easily. Some of the pony breeds tend to be lazy and need motivating. Variety in the work will help to prevent boredom.

CHAPTER 2

EARLY TRAINING

In the previous chapter we considered the conformation of the horse and described the ideal horse for the type of work we wish to do, particularly for competitive purposes. When considering the training of a horse, in particular its early training, we must also understand the way the horse thinks and reacts to certain situations. Although horse psychology is too lengthy a subject to cover in great detail here, it is very important to be aware of the basic instincts of the horse.

TRAINING YOUNG HORSES

It is essential that young horses are only trained by experienced riders and trainers. It is very easy to spoil a young horse forever through carelessness or ignorance. Mistakes that are made in the early days are very difficult or even impossible to put right later and can be very frustrating for everyone concerned. If you are not experienced with youngsters, do not attempt to back or lunge one yourself but seek the help of professionals and work with them. Once a young horse has discovered that it is stronger than its owner, or that it can bully or frighten its owner, it will take full advantage of this and may become dangerous. It is vital that your youngster learns to respect

The horse's mind

People first began to domesticate the horse around the third millennium BC. Through the centuries the domesticated horse has developed a special relationship with humans, first as a partner in work and later in sport or leisure. The horse is designed to move swiftly across the ground and its strong instinct for flight if frightened can cause many problems in training. Horses are very gregarious animals and separation from other horses, especially during weaning from their mother, can make them difficult to handle. Horses kept entirely on their own can become very lonely or even neurotic.

The horse's senses are fairly well developed, particularly those of smell, taste, hearing and touch. It is thought that a 'sixth sense', that of intuition, is also well developed, so that horses often react to people's aggression or fear.

Some people seem to have 'a way with horses'. This is probably due to the fact that the horse reacts well to a calm and gentle personality. When considering the handling and training of the horse you must always remember the three 'Cs': calmness, consideration and consistency.

and obey you from the start.

Once training has begun, it is important to progress at the speed at which the youngster learns. All horses are individuals. Some young horses are well co-ordinated and learn quickly, while others have very short concentration spans and are clumsy and unbalanced. There is no point in establishing a training programme and rushing through the schedule just to get it done. If the horse learns slowly, then take the time that is needed, even if this means that your programme takes much longer than you had envisaged. What matters is that at the end of the training, your horse has learnt how to do things properly and with confidence.

RETRAINING OLDER HORSES

Retraining older horses with vices or behavioural problems is not for the inexperienced or faint-hearted. If you should happen to buy an older horse that requires retraining, you must assess the situation sensibly and decide if you are capable of doing the work or if you should send the horse to an expert. If the horse is simply an older horse that has never been asked to do much except hack out or go hunting now and then, there is probably no reason why you should not succeed providing the horse has a kind temperament and good manners and you take your time over fittening and schooling, remembering that you are asking muscles to work that have lain dormant for years and may be quite stiff to begin with.

On the other hand, problems such as rearing, bolting or throwing serious

tantrums require expert help if you are to avoid being badly hurt or frightened and you might be better not to keep such a horse. No sensible rider wishes to hunt, jump or go across country on a horse that they cannot trust.

DISCIPLINE

Remembering that a good handler is calm, consistent and considerate, we must next discuss the basic discipline of the horse, which is important from the point of view of safety. The horse must be well mannered, both when handled from the ground and when ridden. The word 'discipline' is often incorrectly associated with punishment, although punishment is sometimes necessary and justified. Whether administering punishment or reward, however, it is important to get your timing right. It is pointless to punish a horse more than three seconds after its misdemeanour; it *must* relate the punishment with its crime. When administered, punishment should be short and sharp and should not be aggressive. Horses respond much better to encouragement, so when possible, try to achieve your ends through reward and praise.

HANDLING THE YOUNG HORSE

Handling and basic discipline start at a very early age. Within days of birth, in fact, the foal should have a small headcollar or foal slip put on and be gently lead out to the field with its mother. The foal should first receive attention from the farrier at two

Mare and foal. Discipline should start at an early age.

months, so, prior to this, time should be spent in teaching it how to pick up its feet. It is not really necessary to tie the foal up nor to groom it until it is a yearling. On many large studs, after the initial few months, youngsters get very little handling until they are two or three years old. However, they will still be checked daily by the staff and will become used to people and start to trust them.

At three years old the young horse should be backed and receive some basic training. Some people feel that this is too young. All horses will differ but as the horse gets older, it also becomes stronger and more confident, so it could become more difficult to train. The initial training period will probably only take three months, after which the young horse can be turned away and brought back up into work later when it is four.

BACKING THE YOUNG HORSE

This is sometimes called 'breaking in', although this term tends to suggest that you are breaking the horse's spirit, which is totally wrong. In fact, you are doing completely the opposite, by developing the horse's confidence.

The backing process starts in the stable. The young horse must learn to respect and trust you. It should be tied up when handled and accept basic stable discipline, like moving over when asked and moving back from the door when you enter the stable. A simple snaffle bridle can be introduced in the stable, and some people will leave this on the horse for short periods.

The best way to introduce horses to discipline and to various pieces of

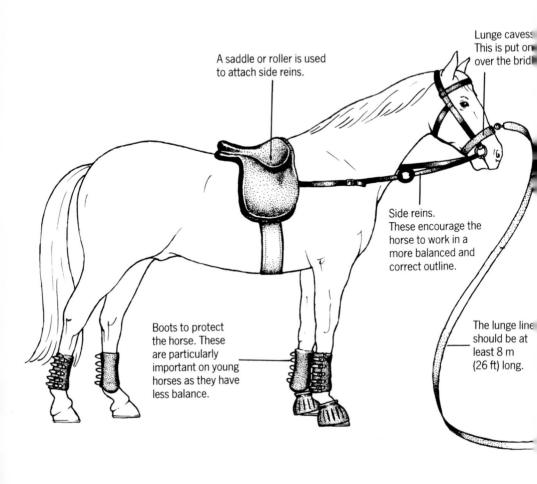

A saddle or roller is used to attach side reins.

Lunge caves
This is put on
over the brid

Side reins.
These encourage the
horse to work in a
more balanced and
correct outline.

Boots to protect
the horse. These
are particularly
important on young
horses as they have
less balance.

The lunge line
should be at
least 8 m
(26 ft) long.

Lungeing equipment.

equipment is on the lunge. The area that you choose to lunge train the horse in must be quiet with good footing. The young horse will usually find it difficult to adjust its balance and is often better working without shoes for the first few weeks.

LUNGEING

Young horses should only be lunged by experienced trainers.

It must be remembered that lungeing is quite stressful, so the young horse must be kept on large circles and worked for only short periods, equally on each rein. Start lungeing by leading the horse around on the circle, using your voice and whip to send it forward and your voice and the lunge line to stop it. Gradually drop back away from the horse and encourage it forward with your voice and whip. Ideally, you want to position yourself so that you are opposite the horse's shoulder, with the horse, lunge line, you and the whip forming a triangle. The whip has two main purposes: to send the horse forward and to keep it out on the circle. Do not be afraid to move around with the horse but be careful not to wander so much that the horse no longer works on a circle. This learned response to your voice will be very helpful when you first mount the horse and start to teach it to respond to your leg and the rein.

Lungeing the horse.

Before using a saddle, it is a good idea to introduce a roller. This is best done in an enclosed, but spacious area in case the horse objects to the feeling of something tight around its girth. After work, leave the roller on in the stable for a while to accustom the horse to the pressure.

The next stage is to replace the roller with a saddle. Some people use an old saddle in case the horse becomes upset. This is fine as long as the saddle fits, so that it will not slip when you want to get on the horse. Saddles with broken trees must not be used, however, as the weight will not be evenly distributed and the horse's back could become bruised.

Side reins should be fitted as soon as the horse seems calm and accepts the work. They should be fitted fairly long – just enough for the young horse to feel a contact.

In the early stages, the young horse should only be worked for about twenty minutes a day; twice if necessary, as its concentration will soon wear out.

MOUNTING FOR THE FIRST TIME

To do this safely, you will require at least two people. The person mounting should lie quietly across the horse's back. It is best to do this from a mounting block or to be legged up by someone. Using the stirrup will come later. Lead the horse around a little to accustom it to the weight on its back. It is well worth remembering that the horse may associate the rider on its back with a predator attacking it, so keep calm and reassure the horse. If all seems well, then the rider

should quietly put their leg over the horse and very slowly sit up. This should be done carefully so as not to startle the horse when it first catches sight of the person sitting up on its back.

This procedure should be repeated for a few days until the horse seems confident and the rider can be led around quietly. When first going into trot, it is best if the rider sits to the trot, holding the saddle and breastplate. This will allow the horse to become accustomed to the rider's weight at the faster pace. As soon as possible, the rider should adopt rising trot.

The next stage is to teach the horse to move forward from the leg and to slow, stop or turn it using the rein. At first, this is done on the lunge when the voice commands taught earlier will now prove useful. The rider co-ordinates the aids with the voice command, backed up with the lunge whip if necessary. When the horse has understood this, the lunge line should be unclipped, leaving the rider to work the horse.

EARLY TRAINING

Whatever you are training the horse to do, be it for dressage, show jumping or another discipline, the early training is fundamentally the same. Each training session should be thought of as a lesson for the horse, in which it is going to be taught and made to understand something. The rider must be clear and confident with the aids and quietly persistent.

The first requirement is that the horse moves freely forward. This means that on a long rein, with the

At first the rider lies across the horse's back.

rider's leg relaxed, the horse will work forward willingly and calmly. Free forward movement is not so much physical as mental. The horse must be encouraged to be mentally prepared to work forward in a free and positive way. In the early days the horse will tend to lose its balance, so it needs to be taught to move forwards from a light leg aid and to slow down, stop or turn from a light rein aid. Horses do vary, but most tend to be either naturally active or naturally lazy.

When the horse has accepted this, it must very quickly be taught to accept a rein contact. Getting the horse to accept the hand is one of the most crucial aspects of training. A horse that is unhappy in its mouth is very difficult to ride and requires an

experienced and quite supple rider. The feeling of a correct contact is very difficult to describe, but it should feel soft and fairly light, yet positive. You should feel that you are able to communicate with the horse and still keep a nice, flexible feeling in the horse's neck. At this stage some people like to use what are known as mouthing bits. The idea is that the horse will play with the keys

A mouthing bit.

Lateral work

Once the youngster has learnt to work freely forward and accept a contact, lateral work should be introduced to help to improve the response to the leg and the horse's suppleness. The first movements taught are *leg yielding* and *turn on the forehand*. Many people do not like turn on the forehand as they feel it makes the horse heavier on the rein. This may be true if it is ridden incorrectly but at this stage the movement is only used to teach the horse to move away from the leg, not to improve its way of going. Turn on the forehand can be taught first from the ground, both in the stable and on the lunge. The horse should be gently nudged just behind its girth and encouraged to move away. This can then be done while the rider applies their inside leg, so that the horse learns to associate the leg with moving away. In the early stages this can cause considerable confusion, as, until this point, the leg has only meant go forward.

The next stage is to ride the horse on an inner track in the school and push it back to the wall with the inside leg. This is the start of leg yielding. The rider may draw the inside leg back at this stage but later the leg should be used just behind the girth where the horse is most sensitive. Leg yielding can be a good loosening exercise for the horse and, if used on circles, it will make the horse softer, more flexible and more responsive.

on the bit and thus soften its jaw. It is all a matter of preference but, as long as the bit is well fitting, it is true to say that it is not the bit but the hands at the other end of the rein that make the difference.

If you are backing a three year old, you may wish to turn it away at this stage. When it comes back up again, you will have to repeat the whole backing procedure, however you should find that the horse will progress much quicker and should now be physically more capable.

TEACHING THE BASIC AIDS

The basic forward driving aid of the leg and the balancing aids of the reins were first taught in the early stages of backing, when the horse was on the lunge. Teaching the horse to work freely forward and accept a contact should be done in the school using easy school figures, such as 20-m circles and transitions from walk to trot. Many people feel that they should not ask too much of a young horse and this is true to a point. However, the young horse must be encouraged to work correctly, in balance and in a round outline from very early on. It should be remembered that a horse can just as quickly learn to go badly as it can learn to go well. If a horse learns to evade the aids, its muscles will develop in an incorrect way and this will allow the evasion to become stronger. If a horse continually evades the aids, it will find it difficult to balance and this will result in it finding the work too difficult, which

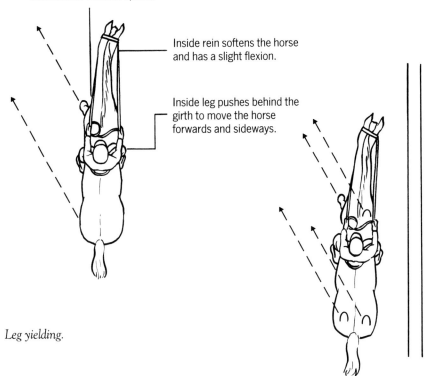

Outside rein controls speed.

Inside rein softens the horse and has a slight flexion.

Inside leg pushes behind the girth to move the horse forwards and sideways.

Leg yielding.

Turn on the forehand.

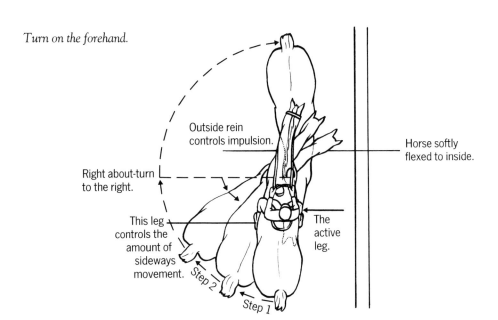

Outside rein controls impulsion.

Horse softly flexed to inside.

Right about-turn to the right.

This leg controls the amount of sideways movement.

The active leg.

Step 2

Step 1

will produce more evasion and possibly tension. Hence, a vicious circle is created.

The young horse must be taught to stretch down on to the bit so that it can engage its hind quarters and use its back. This may mean that, in the early stages, the horse will be a little on its forehand, but this can be corrected when it has learnt to use its back.

HACKING OUT

Hacking should be introduced once the young horse has learnt the basic aids and is reasonably well disciplined. In the early stages it is essential to hack out with another experienced and sensible horse. Before going out on the roads, it is advisable that you work the two horses together in the school. The young horse will often become inattentive when the other horse is in the school, making control more difficult.

When first out on the roads, the young horse should follow the experienced horse. It is a good idea for the rider to wear a bright, reflective vest that warns drivers that this is a young horse.

INTRODUCING THE YOUNG HORSE TO JUMPS

When you are able to balance the young horse in walk, trot and canter, it is ready to start jumping. Whatever the horse finally ends up doing, jumping is a very useful way of developing its strength, suppleness and co-ordination. Jumping is not something that the horse would do naturally, although some horses have

more talent for it than others. It is important, therefore, to remember that jumping is a technique that needs to be taught in a progressive way. This will give the horse confidence and develop boldness. Many horses are ruined as jumpers by lack of jumping training, causing them either to rush their fences or not to jump at all.

The young horse should first be worked over poles on the ground in walk and trot. It is best to start with a single pole and then to progress to two poles 2.7 m (9 ft) apart. This will encourage the horse to trot over the poles and not jump them. When the horse seems confident about this, place the third pole in the middle of the first two. The horse should be encouraged to lower its head and

Stage one – one pole.

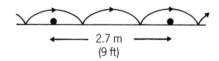

Stage two – two poles.

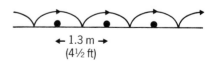

Stage three – three poles.

Trotting poles.

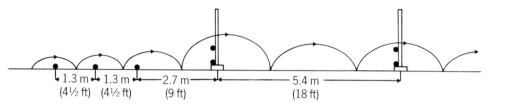

1.3 m   1.3 m   2.7 m   5.4 m
(4½ ft) (4½ ft)   (9 ft)   (18 ft)

A grid of fences.

stretch its neck and back muscles over the poles.

The next stage is to introduce a small cross pole about 2.7 m (9 ft) away from the last trotting pole. This will be the first jump for the horse. The horse will often jump quite awkwardly to start with. However, the rider must remember to sit still and let the horse work out what to do and how to jump. It is vital that the rider does not jab the horse in the mouth. As soon as the horse seems confident, a second fence can be put about 5.4 m (18 ft) away from the first. This could be a straight bar, about 60 cm (2 ft) high. It is important always to use a ground rail with all jumps, because horses judge distance from the ground up. It is also better to fill the fence in well and make it look solid but inviting.

The grid work can be continued until the horse develops a good technique and is confident. The next stage is to progress to small show jump courses and introduce some cross country fences.

This stage of the horse's training can take from six to eight months. The time, patience and attention to detail at this stage will build a foundation of confidence and trust that will ensure continued success. This stage is also the start of the conditioning and fitness process.

CHAPTER 3

FEEDING AND NUTRITION

To maintain good health, it is important to find the correct balance between exercise and feeding. It is equally important for the diet itself to be balanced, so that the horse receives all the necessary nutrients. Good feeding is a science; the knowledge and technology available today should enable us to feed specific amounts of nutrients, to individual horses, which, in top level competition, could make all the difference between winning and losing. This sophisticated technology has become available to every horse owner through the introduction of compound feeds. These are sold either in the form of nuts or as a mix. The feeds are balanced and the mixture will vary depending on the type of work that the horse is to do, e.g. high performance mix would be used for event or racehorses as it has a higher energy and protein content than horse and pony mix. There is nothing weird or wonderful about compound feeds; they are made up of all the same feedstuffs, such as oats and barley, that have been fed for centuries. Their main advantage is that the content is analysed for its nutritional value and balanced with the necessary vitamins and minerals.

FEEDING A BALANCED DIET

To feed a balanced diet, it is first necessary to understand the functions of the various parts of the diet. The importance of each constituent will vary depending on the age of the horse, the type of work it is doing and even the conditions in which it lives.

PROTEIN

Protein has many functions. It forms the body tissues that go to make skin, bones and muscles and also many other cells such as those found in the blood. Proteins are made up of a complex structure of amino acids. Having been absorbed into the digestive system from the feed, they are then metabolised in the liver. The horse manufactures ten amino acids within its own body, but the other ten – twelve amino acids that are required have to be absorbed from the diet. These are called the essential amino acids.

In the adult horse, protein is required basically to perform a repair and maintenance function, so the adult horse only needs about 10 per cent protein in its diet. However, horses that are being put under any kind of stress, for example at endurance competitions, will require higher amounts of protein. The amounts required will also increase if the horse is growing, pregnant, lactating or ill, although veterinary advice should be sought for the latter situation.

The amount of protein stated to be in a feed does not always mean that the horse will actually be receiving that amount. Protein has to be of good quality to be of any nutritional value and this can only be determined by analysis.

CARBOHYDRATE

Carbohydrates provide the energy to fuel the body. This means that carbohydrates must form a significant part of the diet, even for a horse that is not in work, as they provide the necessary energy for such basic functions as breathing and the generating of body heat. However, if fed extra to requirements, carbohydrate is stored as fat. Carbohydrate is found in two main sources: starches and sugars, which are easily utilised, or cellulose, which is a much more complicated structure found in grass and hay. Cellulose is insoluble and is broken down by the bacteria in the caecum and large colon to form what are called volatile fatty acids. These fatty acids are an important source of energy and will be metabolised by the body when required.

FATS (LIPIDS)

Fats are a very valuable source of energy, containing around two and a half times the amount of energy found in carbohydrates. This makes them an excellent nutrient for endurance horses, especially in long distance riding. Because of the high nutritional value of fats, they are only fed in small amounts.

MINERALS

Minerals are divided into two main categories: macro-minerals, which are required in large amounts, and micro-minerals, which are only required in small amounts.

The macro-minerals are calcium, phosphorous, magnesium, potassium, sodium and chloride. The micro-minerals include iron, copper, sulphur, zinc, iodine, selenium and cobalt. Minerals are essential for all body processes and the correct balance is important.

ELECTROLYTES

When dissolved in body fluid, some minerals will ionise, which will result in them having a positive or a negative electrical charge. The minerals will then combine, which is essential for the healthy functioning of the cells, particularly the nerve and muscle cells. These compounds are sometimes referred to as body salts and an example of such an electrolyte is sodium chloride (table salt). Electrolyte fluids can be bought and are often given to a horse at a competition when the horse is rapidly losing body salts through sweating. This loss of fluid can greatly affect the horse's performance, so electrolyte solutions can be invaluable.

VITAMINS

Vitamins have many functions, including aiding growth, tissue repair, digestion and general well being. Some vitamins are synthesised in the hind gut by the same bacteria that break down the feed. These vitamins are classified as water soluble and include vitamins B1–6, B12, B complex and vitamin C. Other vitamins are utilised from the feed and are categorised as fat soluble. These include vitamins A, D, E and K.

Vitamins and minerals can be introduced to the diet in the form of supplements that are fed if the horse has a vitamin deficiency. However, it is impossible to pinpoint which minerals or vitamins are required without having the feed analysed. Overfeeding of supplements can be harmful, so it is best to discuss your horse's feeding requirements with your feed supplier or your vet.

WATER

This is far from being the least important constituent of the feed, as water makes up 50–60 per cent of the horse's body weight. Water quenches the horse's thirst and regulates its body temperature. It is a major constituent of blood, bile, saliva and the digestive juices. For this reason, fresh, clean water must be available to the horse at all times, particularly during hot weather, or when the horse is losing a lot of body fluid through sweating.

Each of the constituents of the diet plays an important role, and the chart above shows the nutritional value of

	DE	CP(%)	Ca(%)	P(%)
Oats	13	11	0.09	0.37
Barley	15	10	0.08	0.40
Maize	16	9	0.05	0.26
Sugar Beet Pulp	12	9	0.75	0.10
Wheat Bran	11	17	0.12	1.45
Horse & Pony Cube	10	10	Balanced	
Competition Cubes	13	13	Balanced	
Good seed hay	10	10	0.50	0.25
Meadow Hay	8	9	0.50	0.25

DE = Digestible Energy which is measured in Megajoules (MJ) per kilogram
CP = Crude Protein
Ca = Calcium
P = Phosphorus
Note: For healthy bone development, the calcium:phosphorus ratio should be 2:1. This should be taken into account when combining feedstuffs. The compound feed manufacturer should balance this for you.

The nutritional value of common feedstuffs.

feedstuffs in common use. The manufacturers of compound feeds use tables just like this to mix and balance their products.

The next stage for the horse owner is to define the type of work that their horse is doing and decide how much feed in total their horse should be getting each day.

CONCENTRATES

This name is given to feeds that contain diet constituents in a concentrated form, for example oats. This means that they can be fed in relatively small amounts.

FIBRE

The main source of fibre for the horse is grass, commonly fed in the form of hay. Fibre is an important part of the diet as it promotes good health in the gut, provides roughage, aids the transportation and breakdown of concentrates and, if of good quality, provides a valuable source of nutrition. There are two main types of hay: *meadow* and *seed hay*. Meadow hay is grown on permanent pasture, which can cause problems, particularly if the pasture has not been well cared for. Poor pasture normally means poor grasses containing weeds which have a low nutritional value and can be poisonous. On the other hand, good quality meadow hay contains large amounts of perennial rye and meadow fescue.

Seed hay is cut from ley grass, which is grass that has been deliberately sown and is usually cut for three years before being ploughed up and replanted. This means that only the good quality grasses with a high nutritional value are used. These are rye, timothy and cocksfoot.

Opposite: **From the left: rye, timothy and cocksfoot grasses.**

The correct concentrate/fibre ratios.

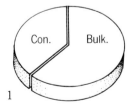
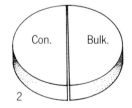
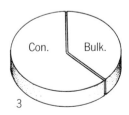

1: horse in light work.
2: horse in general work such as training BHS students or hunting.
3: horse in high-performance work such as three-day eventing or racing.

Total daily intake

The horse should eat around 2.5 per cent of its total body weight in food each day. The body weight can be determined either by using a weigh bridge or by using a special tape that calculates the body weight from a measurement taken around the horse's girth.

The total amount of food is divided into concentrates and fibre, depending on the type of work being done and the horse's level of fitness. It is important to remember that the horse is a grazing animal and that its digestive tract has evolved to cope with this, therefore it *must* receive at least 1 per cent of its daily ration in the form of fibre (i.e. hay).

Horse's body weight = 500 kg (1102 lb)
Total daily intake = 2.5 per cent of 500 = 12.5 kg (27½ lb)

When fit, a hunter would require about 6 kg (13¼ lb) per day in concentrates and 6.5 kg (14⅓ lb) per day in fibre/hay.

FEEDING RULES

Before finally deciding on a feeding programme, certain rules of feeding must be taken into consideration. The horse is naturally a browsing animal; that is to say, its natural habit is to roam on grassland, steadily eating the grass as it wanders. The horse's digestive tract has evolved to cope with this. It has a small stomach, as little breakdown of food takes place there, so the horse should not be fed more than 1½–2 kg (3–4½ lb) in one feed, as it would then pass through the stomach too quickly. It has a long intestine, which is divided into two parts: the small intestine where most of the nutrients are absorbed and the large intestine, where fibre is broken down into volatile fatty acids. The food will stay in the stomach for only a few hours, whereas it remains in the intestine for a couple of days because of the amount of time it takes to break down fibre. For these reasons, it is better to feed little and often, as this simulates the horse's natural feeding pattern and will make it feel more settled.

The digestive tract is very sensitive, particularly the bacteria in the large intestine, so all changes in the diet should be introduced gradually. Also, only high quality feed should be given as any mould will cause problems such as colic. Mould and dust will also have a bad effect on the horse's equally sensitive respiratory tract. Horses are very fastidious and will not eat if they can smell rotting feed, so all utensils should be kept clean.

It is natural for the horse to drink small amounts while it is eating, so fresh water should be constantly available. However, if the horse has been deprived of water for some reason, water should be offered before feeding, as a large draught of water could wash all the feed out of the stomach if given after the feed.

Feed table for a hunter when fit

Total daily intake 12.5 kg (27½ lb) = 6 kg (13¼ lb) concentrates
6.5 kg (14⅓ lb) fibre/hay

7.30 a.m.	1 kg (2¼ lb) hay	4.30 p.m.	2 kg (4½ lb)
8.00 a.m.	1 kg concentrates		concentrates
12.30 a.m.	1 kg hay		2 kg hay
	1 kg concentrates	8.00 p.m.	2 kg concentrates
			2.5 kg (5½ lb) hay

The concentrates would be either oats, mixed with a little sugar beet for taste and chaff to help the horse chew, or a competition or hunter mix. Either of these should meet the feeding requirements, being moderately high in energy and containing about 12 per cent protein.

A small amount of hay is given first thing to activate the digestive system and small feeds are given in the morning to allow for exercise. In the evening, the horse has more time to eat and digest its food, so larger amounts can be given. Feeding small amounts regularly avoids wastage.

MODERN DEVELOPMENTS IN FEEDING

With the scientific knowledge available today, feed is now treated so that the horse gains as much goodness as possible.

Good feeding is in the eye of the trainer!

The best way to tell if your horse is being overfed or underfed is to stand back and take a good look at it. Is it too thin and lacking in energy? Is is too fat and lethargic? Is its coat staring (standing up) or dull? It may be that the horse is receiving large quantities of food but taking no nourishment from it because of a heavy work load, teeth trouble or because the food is contaminated or of poor quality. Ask your vet to take a blood sample and analyse it for mineral deficiencies. Or have the soil in your paddock checked. Discuss with your vet the brand of feed you are using and ask him or her about the advisability of adding something like cod liver oil or garlic powder to the feed. All horses are different and all must be fed as individuals, just like people. When you look at your horse you should see a glossy coat and bright, interested eyes. The horse should look forward to its feed and eat it with relish. As well as checking the tables in the feed charts, you must constantly watch the horse itself with a new eye. That way you will know when something is wrong.

Heat treatments

Some feeds, such as barley, have traditionally been cooked to make them more digestible. In the case of linseed, cooking is essential as it is poisonous in its uncooked form, containing prussic acid. Modern feed processing has made the feed more digestible without reducing its nutritional value, which was always a problem with boiling up feed.

Micronisation

The feed is passed under an infra-red grill, causing the water content in the grain to vaporise. This breaks down the starch and increases its digestibility. Examples of this are micronised barley, maize and peas.

Extrusion

This treatment has been used for several years to treat dog food. The feed is cooked in steam at high temperatures and pressure, causing the starch to swell and crystallise. It is estimated that this increases digestibility by 25 per cent. An example of this is extruded barley.

Steam flaking

The feed is steamed and then rolled and dried. This treatment flakes and splits the grains.

Hay alternatives

It is difficult always to guarantee the nutritional value and quality of hay. The effects of dust and mould on the horse's respiratory system can be very serious.

Haylage/Horsehage

This is made in the same way as good seed hay, containing many of the best grasses. It is allowed to half-dry and is then vacuum packed to allow slow fermentation and to prevent the growth of harmful fungal spores. It has a high energy value, so should be fed with care. Once the packs are opened, they must be fed quickly. It is an excellent source of fibre for horses with respiratory problems.

Silage

Silage is not commonly fed to horses as it is not usually practical for the horse owner to do so. Silage comes in two forms: *clamp silage*, which is stored in a large bay covered with polythene, and *big-bale silage*, which involves baling the half-dry grass into large bales. Be warned, however,

Micronised barley and extruded barley.

Clamp silage.

there have been cases of death when big-bale silage has been fed to horses. Death was caused by excessive acidity being produced when the silage fermented, resulting in botulism, which is a serious form of poisoning.

Hydroponic grass

This is not an alternative to hay but is fed as part of the concentrate ration. Barley seed is grown in a machine

Hydroponic grass.

that creates a controlled environment. It has a high protein content and is very digestible. It is useful for breeding stock but the expense of the cabinets in which it is grown makes it infeasible for more horse owners.

Supplements

There are so many different supplements on the market that it is difficult to name them all. However, they tend to fall into three main categories: high performance, broad spectrum and therapeutic.

High performance

These are for horses that are in hard work, particularly endurance work. They contain proteins to cope with stress and fatty acids to provide energy. They should be fed with care as they can cause serious imbalances in the diet.

Broad spectrum

These contain all the vitamins and minerals required for a healthy diet. It is possible to buy mineral supplements that will help to balance feeds, such as special calcium supplements for oats. Although these are more straightforward to feed than high performance supplements, they should not be overfed as imbalances may still be caused.

Therapeutic

Many different supplements come under this heading, ranging from homoeopathic to special protein mixtures.

It is best to seek veterinary advice before using supplements. Never mix supplements together, as this could result in a dangerous cocktail.

CHAPTER 4

A GENERAL CONDITIONING PROGRAMME

A horse that is in good condition is also in good health. For all horses, but particularly those that are stabled, the correct balance of feeding and exercise will promote good health and condition. When people talk about fitness and condition, they are often referring to the amount of muscle and fat that the horse is carrying. This can sometimes lead to confusion as people tend to think that a fit horse should be thin. This is not the case. A very fit racehorse is lean, but carries a lot of muscle, so it must be fed enough to give it all the nutrients it requires to

A fit horse is lean and well muscled.

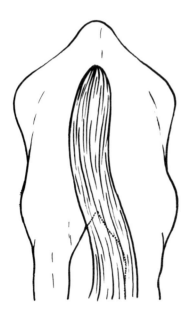
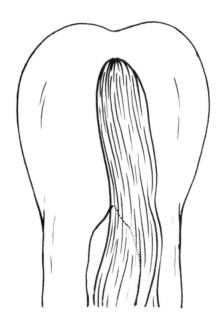

Poor hind quarters.

Obese hind quarters.

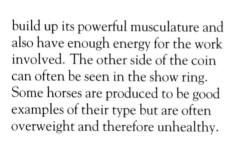

build up its powerful musculature and also have enough energy for the work involved. The other side of the coin can often be seen in the show ring. Some horses are produced to be good examples of their type but are often overweight and therefore unhealthy.

CONDITION SCORING

Assessing condition does take experience but a useful guide can be to score the horse from 0–5 to ascertain if it is carrying enough weight and muscle.

The areas to be assessed are the horse's neck, spine, ribs, hips and hind quarters. These should be assessed by standing directly behind and then in front of the horse and looking down its body, and also by touch. If the skeletal frame is visible, the horse is in fairly poor condition.

The condition of the horse will also reflect its general health – being either too thin or too fat is unhealthy. However, sometimes a horse in good condition can still be suffering from ill health, so you must be aware of the signs of health.

THE HEALTHY HORSE

The signs of good health can be categorised under two main headings: visual signs of health and internal signs of health.

Visual signs

- **Expression:** This should be alert. Horses are naturally inquisitive, so any dullness or disinterest may signify ill health.

- **Respiration:** If the horse is blowing – the breathing is laboured or noisy – then the horse is in distress. The normal

Condition score

0 POOR

Neck: Lacking any muscle. Bone structure visible. Top line looks weak.

Spine: Spinal processes project prominently.

Ribs: Very prominent. Can be seen all the way up to the top of the back.

Hips: Very prominent. No fat tissue can be felt.

Quarters: Drop away to the hips. Bone structure is clearly visible.

1 THIN

Neck: Lacking muscle and top line, but bone structure not visible. Bones can be felt.

Spine: Slight fat covering on spinal processes, although still visible.

Ribs: Slight fat covering, but still visible.

Hips: Prominent, but have a slight fat covering.

Quarters: Fall away from spine. Tailhead prominent.

2 MODERATE

Neck: Not obviously thin. Neck blends into shoulders.

Spine: Spinal processes not visible, but easily felt. Withers are rounded.

Ribs: Not visible, but easily felt.

Hips: Only slightly prominent.

Quarters: Much rounder.

3 GOOD CONDITION

Neck: Blends well into shoulders and withers. Some fat deposited along the sides of the shoulders and neck.

Spine: Back flat.

Ribs: Fat covering over ribs feels spongy.

Hips: Not prominent, but can be felt.

Quarters: Rounded.

4 FAT

Neck: Neck noticeably thickened, with fat deposits along the side of neck.

Spine: Back flat, with a slight crease along spine.

Ribs: Well covered, cannot be felt unless a lot of pressure is applied.

Hips: Cannot be felt.

Quarters: Inner thigh has fat deposited on it. Fat deposited over the top of the quarters, causing a crease along the croup.

5 OBESE

Neck: Fat deposited in front of the withers and along the top and sides of the neck, giving a crest.

Spine: Back has a deep groove running along the spine.

Ribs: Cannot be felt. Large patches of fat deposited.

Hips: Not discernible.

Quarters: Large deposits of fat. Deep groove along the croup.

Each area should be scored. A horse in ideal condition should score 3 for each area.

respiration for an adult horse is eight to sixteen breaths per minute. Coughing is a sign of disease. It is the body's natural reflex action to irritation of the respiratory tract. This could be due to either dust or infection.

U Nostrils: These should be clear and clean of discharge. A white-coloured mucous discharge usually signifies some dust irritation. Yellow mucous discharge, especially if copious, signifies infection or disease.

U Eyes: These should be clear, bright and shiny.

U Stance: The horse should be standing evenly on all four limbs. It is quite natural for horses to rest a hind limb, but not a forelimb. Horses rest their forelimbs by pointing them out in front of their body. If the horse is standing tucked up, possibly holding its tail in the air, this is a sign of pain.

U Coat: The coat shows the general condition of the horse, as it reflects the condition of the skin. It should be flat and shiny. Sweating is a sign of raised temperature, pain or discomfort.

U Appetite: A sure sign that a horse is feeling unwell is if it leaves its food. Horses' feeding habits vary but, generally, they

Pointing a foreleg.

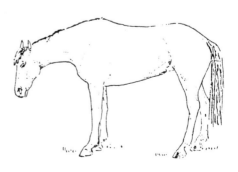

Looking tucked up.

43

will have a good appetite and eagerly await their food.

⋃ **The stable:** The conditions of the bedding and the droppings passed by the horse can tell you a lot about the horse's health. If the bed is badly churned up, it signifies that the horse has had a restless night. This could be due to colic, or possibly the horse has been cast. Look around the walls for any tell tale scoring, which would have been caused by the thrashing hooves as the horse tried to free itself. It may have injured itself doing this, so check it over carefully. The droppings should be neither too hard nor too loose. There should be no obvious smell. A horse will normally produce between eight and twelve piles of droppings every twelve hours. The number and consistency of the droppings can tell you a lot about the state of health of the horse's very sensitive digestive tract. Any abnormalities should be monitored; if they last for more than 24 hours, your veterinary surgeon should be consulted.

Internal signs

These should only be investigated if any of the visual signs are abnormal. All abnormalities will help your vet to diagnose the problem.

⋃ **Temperature:** This is taken by placing a thermometer in the horse's rectum and holding it there for a couple of minutes. It is better to lubricate the thermometer with petroleum jelly

or another veterinary lubricant. The normal temperature should be around 38°C or 101.5°F. The vet should be consulted if there is any rise in temperature.

⋃ **Pulse:** The normal pulse of a horse at rest is between 36 to 40 beats per minute. During work it can go as high as 200 beats per minute. The best way to take the pulse is by placing a stethoscope on the left-hand side of the girth area, about 15 cm (6 in) in from the elbow. Alternatively, you can feel the pulse of the facial artery where it crosses the jaw bone. A rapid pulse signifies pain. Any abnormalities should be reported to your vet.

⋃ **Respiration:** This should be eight to sixteen breaths per minute at

Taking the pulse at the facial artery.

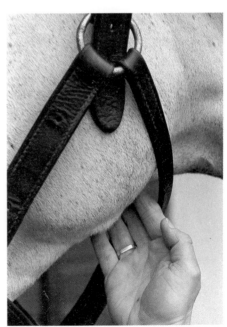

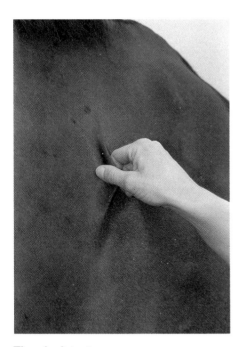

The pinch test.

With the competition horse, dehydration can cause real problems. During work, the horse loses large amounts of body fluid in sweat. A simple test to check for dehydration is to pinch a flap of skin, usually on the neck. If it is slow to recover, this is a sign that the horse is dehydrated.

Mucous membranes
For the purpose of examination, the membranes of the inner lining of the eyelids are the easiest to look at. Normally they should be a salmon-pink colour. Pale membranes may signify anaemia, bright red membranes may signify fever and yellow membranes may signify a liver complaint.

Legs and hooves
The legs and feet should be checked daily, first thing in the morning and then again after work. The legs and hooves should be cold and free from any swelling. Any heat or swelling will signify inflammation or infection. Heat in the legs should always be treated with caution as a minor injury could become serious if the horse is worked with it.

Urine
This should be clear. Any discoloration can signify disorder or disease.

FITNESS TRAINING

The conditioning programme
In this book, there are chapters on fitness and training for eventing, dressage, show jumping and hunting.

rest. When a horse is working, its respiration can go as high as 100 breaths per minute. The respiration is counted by watching the rise *and* fall of the horse's flanks.

It is important to monitor the horse's normal TPR (temperature, pulse and respiration) and keep a record. When you know what is normal, you will also know when it is abnormal.

∪ **Skin:** This should run smoothly and freely over the body. The skin and coat can be thought of as a mirror that reflects the horse's health. If the skin is in generally poor condition, this is also true of the health of the horse. The skin can be affected by many diseases, not just those specific to the skin.

These are all fairly diverse and require different levels and types of fitness. However, the body should first of all be conditioned before any real stress is placed on it, so a basic six–eight-week conditioning process can be used for all these disciplines before introducing specific training programmes. During this first six–eight weeks we introduce work that conditions and therefore strengthens the connective tissue, namely the skin, tendons, muscles, ligaments and bones. Basically, fitness training works by inducing stress on the body and therefore causing physiological changes to take place. Specific types of work will create specific changes. It is important to remember that overstressing the body causes damage. This first six weeks' work is very important to lessen the risks of overstressing the horse.

A six-week programme

This programme is a suitable start for a horse that has been in little or no work. At this stage the horse is in what is known as soft condition. (Feeding and nutrition are covered in more depth in the next chapter, but references are also made in this chapter where relevant. The management of the horse is also mentioned, as success depends on good stable management.)

Remember to keep the work varied and interesting to avoid boredom and keep the horse alert to your aids. If you think the horse is becoming stale and switched off through doing the same thing each day, try to ring the changes a little by taking a different route or going out alone or with a companion. Mix relaxation with hard work and do not go on and on grinding away at something until the horse becomes bored or overtired. Boredom can show up as nappiness. Try to be aware of the difference between cheerful high spirits and naughtiness and remember to ride through your problems, not give in to them as you will only have to face them again another day.

Week One

The horse should spend the first week in walk on hard level surfaces such as roads. At the beginning of the week you may only work the horse for twenty minutes. But by the end of the week it should be walking for up to one hour. Some people also lunge the horse in the early stages. Lungeing is far more stressful than work on straight lines, however, so it should really only be used if the horse is likely to object to having the rider on straightaway. Walking on the roads starts to condition the muscles, bones, ligaments and tendons. The weight of the rider helps to develop the horse's strength, and wearing tack will start to harden the skin. It is a good idea to help the skin to harden by bathing the saddle area with a saline solution (6 g or 1 teaspoon salt to half a litre or 1 pt water). This area should be checked daily for any rubs. The legs should also be checked daily for heat and the shoes checked for wear.

At this stage, the horse should be on a high-fibre diet, which should consist of good quality hay and a small amount of concentrates. If the horse has been living out in the field, it may now come in for short periods each day. This means that the diet is being changed, and care must be taken to introduce new feeds slowly, so as not to upset the bacteria that live in the caecum and large colon. These bacteria break down foodstuffs, particularly the cellulose in grass and hay. If the diet is changed suddenly, particularly if the amount of hay is dropped and the concentrate ration increased, these essential bacteria will be destroyed.

Week Two

The walking exercise should be increased to one hour. You should start to include gradual inclines by the end of the week. Uphill work will help to get the horse fit without stressing its legs unduly. It will also increase its respiration and heart rate, which will help to condition the heart and lungs.

You should keep a careful eye on the horse's legs for any signs of heat and continue to wash its tack areas with saline solution. You may wish to increase the concentrate ration a little, and if the horse is carrying a lot of weight, cut the hay ration.

Week Three

The horse should be worked for one and a half hours daily. The walk should be active and the horse encouraged to work in a correct outline. There is a definite difference between hacking and fitness training. Hacking is often a form of relaxation for the horse and rider, so the horse will probably be on a long rein for most of the time. When the horse is being fittened, it must work harder and use the correct muscles. This will make it much stronger, so that it will find the later work in the programme

easier. Hill work should be used more and more.

The horse's shoes will need checking as they will probably be worn. If the horse has been living out, it should now be in all the time, although it may be going out in the field for a couple of hours' relaxation a day.

Week Four

The work can be increased to two hours daily, although this is not necessary unless you are going to be eventing or hunting. Some trot work can be introduced on level going, but only in two–three minute bursts. This is preferable to work at the faster gaits on soft going but should not be done on roads, in order to lessen the amount of concussion on the horse's legs and feet.

Week Five

From now on the length of time spent working the horse remains the same at two hours per day; only the type of work becomes more difficult. More trot should be introduced, so that it takes up about 15–20 minutes of the programme. It should still only be done in two–three minute bursts, although more trot up inclines should be done. A short, steady canter can be done on level, soft ground.

Week Six

The work is very much the same as week five. You may increase the trotting time to 20–25 minutes and start to canter up slight inclines.

Physiological changes that take place in the body

The first six weeks will begin to

prepare and strengthen the body. The work is very controlled and specific so that the body has time to adapt and change without damage. Looking at the work done so far, we can see how this is done.

Walking on the roads

The slight concussive effect caused by the horse walking on the hard road causes the bones to strengthen and remodel. Bone is made up of a fibrous protein called collagen. On to this is encrusted the minerals calcium and phosphorus, which give the bones their density. Bone is a living structure that adapts to any changes such as increased stress. Remodelling is the term used to describe how bone changes, particularly when put under stress. The bone will thicken and become denser and stronger. The muscles and tendons pull and move the bones, so they need to be

strengthened and toned up as well. The tendons in particular will respond to slow work on a hard surface. Tendons are also made of collagen, laid down in long bundles of fibres that are joined together. The collagen will replenish itself as it becomes older and weaker. In the working horse, this replenishment takes place more often. The younger the collagen, the stronger it is and the better the tendons are able to cope with stress and strain.

Trot work

As mentioned earlier, it is better to do as much trot work as possible on softer ground. Short trots on the road are useful, but too much trot work, particularly in the early stages of the programme, could overstress the bones and cause damage. When the horse first walks forward, its heart rate will double. It will increase again

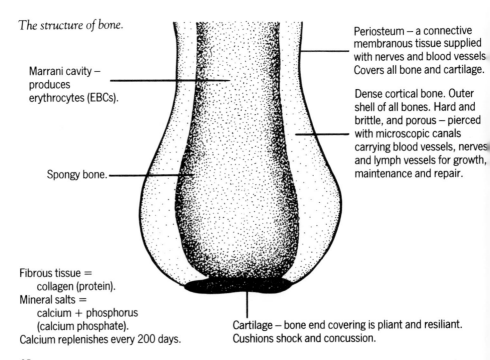

The structure of bone.

Marrani cavity – produces erythrocytes (EBCs).

Spongy bone.

Periosteum – a connective membranous tissue supplied with nerves and blood vessels. Covers all bone and cartilage.

Dense cortical bone. Outer shell of all bones. Hard and brittle, and porous – pierced with microscopic canals carrying blood vessels, nerves and lymph vessels for growth, maintenance and repair.

Fibrous tissue = collagen (protein).
Mineral salts = calcium + phosphorus (calcium phosphate).
Calcium replenishes every 200 days.

Cartilage – bone end covering is pliant and resiliant. Cushions shock and concussion.

The structure of a tendon in cross-section.

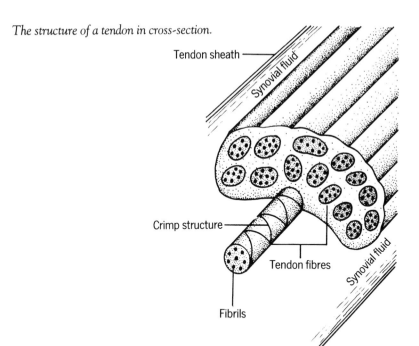

Tendon sheath

Synovial fluid

Crimp structure

Tendon fibres

Synovial fluid

Fibrils

The structure of muscle.

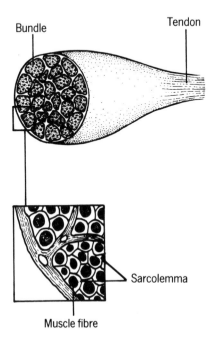

Bundle

Tendon

Sarcolemma

Muscle fibre

when the horse begins to trot, so trot work starts to strengthen the muscular heart and increase the efficiency of the lungs and diaphragm. The muscles, bones and tendons are infiltrated by blood vessels. The blood carries nutrients round the body and, when the horse is working, will carry nutrients and oxygen to fuel the muscles and carry waste products away. As the work becomes more demanding, the rate of efficiency at which this is done must increase. Work at the faster gaits will encourage this by increasing respiration and reclaiming all the air sacs (alveoli) in the lungs, some of which may not have been used while the horse was not working, so that more oxygen can be inhaled and more waste products (carbon dioxide) can be exhaled. The tiny blood vessels (capillaries), that transport the oxygen to the muscles and take the waste away, will increase in number as unused capillaries are brought back into use.

Canter Work
Canter work is particularly useful for developing muscle strength. All the work done so far will help to develop muscles, but canter is the only one of the three paces in which the horse moves asymmetrically. This means that it uses different muscles, depending on whether it is working in left canter or right canter. Horses tend to be weaker on one side than the other, so you can strengthen specific muscles of a horse that is, for example, weaker on the left, by cantering on the left leg more often than the right.

CHAPTER 5

FITNESS AND TRAINING FOR DRESSAGE

For many people, the word 'dressage' tends to conjure up a picture of riding endless circles. One often hears riders complaining that they have to endure the boredom of dressage so that they can then jump and go across country, while others only show jump because they say they can't understand dressage. What this means is that they have misunderstood the very purpose of dressage and, possibly, if it were called 'gymnastic training' instead, which is how the word roughly translates into English, more people would realise the importance of dressage in the general training of all competition horses.

Dressage is the development of the horse's physique and, therefore, its ability to perform. Correct training should encourage this and also develop the horse's paces, making it more flexible, supple and loose. However, none of this is possible unless the horse is calm; calmness results from the horse having confidence in its rider and confidence results from a logical and systematic training programme. All of these qualities are required in every discipline, even for a horse that just

hacks out, as surely it is more pleasurable to ride a well-balanced and co-operative horse. Therefore, it is true to say that dressage forms the solid base of all training.

This point was made in Chapter 2, when the early training of the horse was explained. A young show jumper should receive the same basic schooling as a young dressage horse, although their later training will differ.

BASIC SCHOOLING FOR DRESSAGE

In this chapter we shall discuss the training of a horse to work at BHS Novice level dressage. This requires that the horse is working on the bit and in a correct outline so that it can perform various movements accurately in free walk, medium walk, working trot and working canter. Looking at these requirements more closely will help to explain the schooling programme.

ON THE BIT

This very term tends to be the first problem in the training of many horses. By definition, the term is used to describe a horse that has accepted the bit with a light and soft contact, with a steady head and no resistance being offered to the rider. The horse's hocks must be carrying a little more weight and this requires them to be more underneath the horse.

However, to achieve the effect of a horse working with its head and neck in a shorter form often means that the rider simply pulls against the horse's mouth and literally drags the horse's head in, which causes many problems. It would be better to say that the horse should be worked *to* the bit or *to* the bridle. This is a much more accurate description, as to work on the bit correctly requires the horse to work forward freely from the rider's leg into a rein contact that encourages it to feel secure and relaxed and so that it can be steadied should it rush and lose its balance. The horse that is working on the bit correctly is moving actively forward, with its hind feet stepping further underneath its body, so that it works free from tension through its back and neck into the rein which it

A horse working short and hollow.

A good working outline the horse is working correctly on the bit.

A collected outline.

accepts with it poll as the highest point and its head just slightly in front of the vertical.

It is also important to explain the terms '*engagement*' and '*outline*'. The term 'engagement' is used to describe the amount of weight the horse carries on its hind legs. When the horse steps into the tracks left by its forefeet with its hind feet, it is said to be 'tracking up'. This is done quite naturally but when the rider takes a rein contact the horse may tend to take shorter steps behind, so the rider must activate it with their legs. If the horse accepts the bit and its hind legs are engaged, it is on the bit and working in an outline. It is important to note that the horse's outline can differ, depending on its level of training. There are working, collected, medium and extended outlines; working being the easiest and collected and extended the most difficult. The difference between the working and collected outlines is best explained by studying the diagrams show above.

THE PACES

◡ **Free walk** The walk has a four-time beat and, to be correct, is in an even rhythm. It is said that the walk accurately reflects the standard of the horse's training as this is the pace that is ruined most by tension. A free walk allows the horse complete freedom of the neck, so it does not remain on the bit. It should lower and stretch its neck but remain in the same rhythm. Horses that raise their head and rush in the free walk are tense and unhappy. This is probably because they have not learnt to accept a contact confidently. A horse with a good walk will form a 'V' with the foreleg and hind leg on the same side.

◡ **Medium walk** Other than the free walk, there are collected, medium and extended walks. These walks differ from the free walk in that they all require the horse to be on the bit. The medium walk is of moderate extension. This means that the hind feet step into or just over the tracks left by the forefeet and it is the easiest of the three. (Unlike the other paces, there is no working walk.) In the collected walk, the horse must carry much more weight on its hind quarters and lighten its forehand. This results in shorter but more elevated steps. The extended walk requires engagement and extension, which results from the horse being more active. The medium walk is between the two. With correct training, the

rhythm will be the same in all four types of walk.

◡ **Working trot** This is the easiest of the different types of trot, and requires the horse to be on the bit and in a correct outline. The horse must be balanced and working in an even two-time-beat rhythm. At Novice level, the horse will be asked to lengthen its stride at working trot. When doing this, it should take longer steps, not quicker steps; hurrying denotes loss of balance.

◡ **Working canter** The requirements for working canter are similar to working trot except that canter has a three-time beat. Horses tend to be more on their forehand in canter and it is usually the last pace to become properly balanced. The footfalls of the canter differ, depending on which foreleg is leading, so to be properly balanced the horse must lead with the left foreleg on the left rein and *vice versa* on the right. Horses tend to favour one leading leg, so some suppleness will need to be developed on circles to help to correct this.

SUPPLING THE HORSE

It is important to work on suppling exercises to make the horse equally supple on each rein. Begin with shallow loops up the long sides of the school and then go on to circles and serpentines, first large ones, then smaller ones. Do the same amount of work on each rein – do not just grind away at the horse's stiffer side, making its muscles ache.

PROBLEMS

If the horse tends to rush, try working on 15–20-m circles and incorporate lots of half-halts and transitions until the horse comes off its forehand and learns to balance and carry itself. Make sure that you are riding from leg into hand, so that your leg aid is the stronger and the horse is not tempted to lean on your hand. If it does this, keep giving and taking the rein until the horse learns to carry itself.

If the horse is slow to respond to your leg aids, use the schooling whip. There is no point in thumping away at the horse's side. It must learn to respond to the lightest of leg aids. Transitions through halt may help to make the horse listen to you. Vary the work and the exercises to prevent boredom. Do not resort to spurs just because your legs get tired and do not ride a young horse in spurs. Instead, teach it to respond to your leg aids.

If you constantly get the wrong canter lead, check your own position. Are you sitting crookedly? Are your aids clear? Ask for canter coming into a corner off the long side of the school or on a circle. Try leg yielding from a small circle out on to a larger one and then ask for canter. When out hacking, ask for a particular canter lead. If you do not get it, bring the horse back to trot and ask again.

Every now and then have a lesson with a more experienced teacher. They will often be able to spot faults and solve problems caused by your own riding position. It is easy to slip into bad habits if no one is watching you.

PREPARING FOR COMPETITION

Dressage does require a level of fitness, especially as the horse works up the levels to Advanced. If you liken dressage to gymnastics, then you will understand that the suppleness and strength required to perform well require regular, if not daily, exercise. A mistake often made by inexperienced people is the assumption that working on a circle is not stressful or tiring. On the contrary, it is quite difficult for the horse, especially if it is unfit. A tired horse will not co-ordinate its movements, and therefore will be difficult to balance and train. This can mean that the rider becomes frustrated with the horse and the horse then becomes tense and upset,

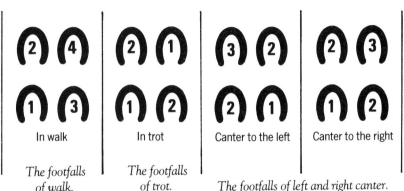

In walk   In trot   Canter to the left   Canter to the right

The footfalls of walk.   *The footfalls of trot.*   *The footfalls of left and right canter.*

none of which makes for good dressage training. If the horse is unfit, it should spend at least four or five weeks doing the sort of work described in Chapter 4. This will make it strong enough to cope with the dressage schooling. A schooling programme will need to be developed to teach the horse how to work correctly and also exercise it so that it becomes stronger and more able to perform well. The following programme is quite useful for a novice horse.

U Walk the horse on a long, loose rein. It should walk actively forward, without being tense, but without you having to urge it forward. This is free forward movement. If the horse will not work forward on a loose rein, it will certainly not work forward with a rein contact. If the horse is idle, tap it with the schooling whip, sharply if necessary, to wake it up.

U Take up a rein contact. As you do this you will need to apply more leg, as the horse may hesitate as it feels the contact in its mouth. The horse should relax its jaw, poll, neck and back and accept the bit. If it does not, keep your leg on and softly encourage the horse to relax by putting more pressure on the reins. As soon as it softens, lighten the contact to reward it, but not so much that it comes above the bit again.

U Do not walk the horse for too long; push it into trot, keeping the nice contact that you have achieved.

U Work in rising trot so that the horse can loosen its back and lengthen its stride. It should be active, but not rushing; a steady rhythm is important.

U Work on 20-m circles, encouraging the horse to relax to the inside rein and take the outside rein from your inside leg. If the horse is heavy on the inside rein, decrease the size of the circle and push the horse out again with your inside leg, backed up with the whip if it is slow to respond. Be careful not to let the horse rush. Keep doing this until the horse takes the outside rein.

U When the trot feels balanced and the horse has a good contact on the rein, canter. You may find it better to adopt a more forward position to start with as this will also help to loosen the horse's back. Ride trot/canter transitions until the horse feels responsive and active. Try to maintain the rhythm of the trot and canter. If the horse rushes in the transitions, steady it with the rein. Transitions will encourage the horse to bring more weight on to its hind legs.

U Ride more transitions, including walk to trot and trot to walk. This will help to engage the hocks and improve the horse's balance. Try to keep a soft contact throughout the transitions as this will improve the outline and encourage the horse to work on to the bit.

U When the horse has accepted these transitions, try some half-halts. To make a half-halt, apply the same aids as for a downward transition but then, when you feel the horse steadying, apply more leg and soften the hand. Half-halts have the same effect as a transition but they rebalance and collect the horse even more. When a horse has learnt to respond to the half-halt, it will improve all the other work, including the transitions as the horse will be better balanced with its hocks more engaged. Half-halts should be applied as soon as you feel the horse losing balance or impulsion, which could be quite often, perhaps even every few strides.

↻ Practise some of the movements from your tests as these are designed to help to improve the horse and test its obedience and suppleness.

↻ Finish the work by allowing the rein and letting the horse stretch down. Maintain the same rhythm, but encourage the horse to stretch through its back. This will loosen it and allow blood back into its tired muscles. It is important to remember that muscles can soon tire and feel cramped. Stretching will help to relieve this.

Study the tests you will be riding until you can ride the movements but do not work through tests continually or else the horse will begin to anticipate the movements. Remember that the horse will respond well to the three 'Cs': calmness, consideration and consistency. When you school

the horse, respond to what you feel is happening each time with logical exercises. For example, if the horse feels heavy on one rein and unresponsive to the leg, use leg yield, turn on the forehand and circles to improve it. Do not accept second best. If the horse is unresponsive, tap it with the schooling whip. If it rushes, steady it with the leg and rein. Keep working it like this until it understands what you want. Most horses only become difficult to ride because they either don't understand or have taken command of the rider.

COMPETING

Once you have entered a competition, do not forget to make a note of when to telephone for your starting time. When you arrive at the competition, go to the secretary and report that you intend to compete.

Working in
Allow plenty of time to work your horse in. Follow the same programme that you use at home. All horses react differently at competitions, so be prepared to be patient. However, you should quietly insist that the horse gives you the same level of work that it would at home. If the horse is very excitable, it may be worth while riding it in early and then bring it out again before you compete. You will find that you need to experiment until you discover the routine that suits you best. The horse should settle more as it goes to more competitions.

Riding the test
When you first start competing, it is a good idea to ride the test at home a

Rider working in. When working in, use the same progamme that you use at home.

few times so that you can practise the movements and learn the test. When you compete, you can have someone call out or command the test for you, but don't rely totally on them. It is difficult enough to concentrate on riding the test without having to listen to what the commander is saying. They should only be there to prompt you if you forget the test. It is difficult to give advice on riding tests, but the following pointers may help:

U Try to relax. You will ride better.

U Try not to rush through the test. You will keep the horse in better balance if the rhythm is steady.

U Don't be afraid to correct the horse if it is being disobedient.

You should think of the test as a schooling session.

U Be as accurate as possible, but not at the expense of spoiling the way the horse is working. Keep the test smooth and flowing; it will give a better impression. Accuracy will have to be worked on at home.

RULES AND REGULATIONS

All competitions have rules that must be adhered to. Competitions that are affiliated to the British Horse Society abide by the rules set down by the BHS. You have to be a member of the BHS to compete and your horse must be registered with the BHS.

Tack and equipment at Preliminary and Novice level

* permitted
x not permitted
c compulsory

English or continental style
   saddle *
Western saddle x
Snaffle bridle *
Double bridle x
Martingale x
Boots or bandages x (they are
   allowed, however, when
   working in)
Running or draw reins x

Note: You may only work the horse
in wearing the tack in which you
will ride it. However, the horse
may be lunged in side reins. Only
cavesson, drop or flash nosebands
are allowed.

Studs

At this level, tests are often ridden on
grass. It is advisable to fit studs,
preferably all round, to give the horse
better grip. If it feels that the footing
is slippery, it will not work well.

Rider's dress

Riding hat c
Breeches c (must be beige, cream or
   white)
Gloves c (must be light coloured)
Boots c (must be black or brown.
   Jodphur boots are acceptable)
Riding jacket c (may be blue, black
   or tweed)
Tie *
Stock *

Note: Rules for Pony Club
competitions vary, so check before
going.

CHAPTER 6

FITNESS AND TRAINING FOR SHOW JUMPING

Jumping is not a natural instinct for the horse. In the wild, the horse would only jump if fleeing from a predator. Some horses have more jumping ability than others, but all horses have to be taught how to jump correctly. This having been said, the rider should encourage every horse to jump to the best of its natural ability, which means that the training programme should be tailored to suit each individual horse. Jump training will help to enhance the horse's athletic ability and, combined with basic dressage schooling, will develop a horse's strength, suppleness and agility. To understand the training programme, we must first be aware of how the horse should be encouraged to jump.

PREPARING FOR COMPETITION

The level of training and fitness required for jumping is a little more exacting than for dressage. This is because the horse requires the same basic fitness that was explained in Chapter 4, plus the basic dressage training explained in Chapter 5. The

stronger the horse is, the better its technique and co-ordination will be. The horse must be balanced and working in a correct outline to enable it to develop a correct jumping technique. However, jumping can also be used to improve dressage training and *vice versa*. Jumping should be introduced as soon as the rider is able to balance the horse.

IMPROVING THE HORSE'S NATURAL JUMPING TECHNIQUE

One of the main aims of your training programme is to develop the horse's confidence. This will encourage it to relax and it will then soften its neck and back muscles and use itself better. This is done by improving the horse's strength and co-ordination. It is important to emphasise that correct jump training develops the horse's natural ability. It is very tempting, especially in the early stages, for the rider to interfere and influence the horse too much. This will result in the horse relying on the rider and, because it will not develop the confidence to use itself, it will only be as brave or as clever as its rider. Particularly in the early stages, the exercises used should aim to develop the horse's strength and self-confidence.

GRIDWORK

This will develop technique, strength, co-ordination and confidence. The following progressive programme will help to ensure this.

Trotting poles

These are used to introduce the horse to poles and to develop its confidence to work over them. When the poles are at the correct distance (approx. 1.3 m or 4½ ft), the horse will place its foot in the middle of the space between the poles. Poles will also help to regulate the horse's rhythm, lengthen or shorten its stride (depending on the distance) and the action of picking up its legs to clear the poles will help to loosen its back and joints. It is important to keep a steady rhythm over the poles and, when the horse feels relaxed, soften the contact to allow the horse freedom in its head and neck as it goes over them. Later, the poles can

be raised slightly. This will help to strengthen the horse but, as it is quite tiring, it should be done with care.

Related fences

From the trotting poles, you can progress into a fence and then into a number of fences in succession. The distances between the fences can be varied to ask different questions of the horse and the fences themselves can be built to help to improve the shape the horse makes over the fence. It is best to approach the line of fences in trot to start with, especially with a young or inexperienced horse, as you will be able to keep it better balanced. The canter can tend to become rather onward bound and, if not properly balanced, this will make the horse jump flat. Key points to remember are:

∪ Build the grids up gradually.

∪ Keep the fences low and simple until the horse is confident.

∪ Always use a ground line so that the horse is encouraged to look at the bottom of the fence. This will improve its take off.

∪ Have someone on the ground to adjust the distances between fences if necessary. Horses' strides differ and incorrect distances do more harm than good.

A simple grid of fences.

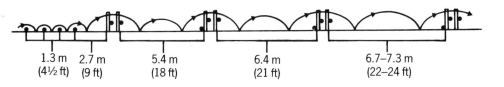

1.3 m	2.7 m	5.4 m	6.4 m	6.7–7.3 m
(4½ ft)	(9 ft)	(18 ft)	(21 ft)	(22–24 ft)

Approach in trot

The phases of jumping

Jumping a fence can be broken down into seven phases: preparation, approach, take off, flight, descent, landing and get-away.

Phase one – preparation

The horse must be balanced and active. The preparation and approach to the fence will determine the point of take off. The horse will lose sight of the fence about one stride before take off, so it is then jumping from memory. This happens because the horse's eyes are set on the side of its face and the fence will go out of its vision as it comes close to it. Nevertheless, if the horse is working in a balanced stride, it will still make a good approach.

Phase two – approach

This links very closely to phase one. On the approach, the horse should keep the same rhythm and stride so that it has the confidence to take off in the correct place. The stride will only need to be altered on the approach if the preparation was poor. This reinforces the importance of good preparation, as altering a stride on the approach, even if it is bad, will undermine a horse's confidence.

Phase three – take off

The horse will slightly lower its head in the last stride to bring its hocks

Placing poles

These can be used instead of trotting poles as the horse becomes better balanced. They are very useful when you start to jump from canter. Their purpose is to place the horse at the correct point of take off, which is usually closer to the fence than the point at which the horse would naturally jump. The closer a horse gets to the fence, the more power it can employ to jump upwards and forwards. This will be particularly valuable when the horse starts to jump spread fences. A common problem is for a horse to stand off and more underneath it, which enables it to spring off the ground. To take off, the horse will lift its neck to bring its forehand up from the ground. As it does so, it will propel itself upwards and forwards from its hind legs.

Phase four – flight

With good technique, the horse will fold its forelegs up and stretch its neck forwards. As it reaches the top of the jump, it should form an arc with its body, its withers coming up as its neck stretches forwards and down. This will enable it to tuck its hind legs up to clear the fence. This rounded shape in jumping is called a *bascule*.

Phase five – descent

The horse will straighten its forelegs to meet the ground. It will raise its head again to rebalance itself and enable it to shift its weight on to its hind quarters when it lands.

Phase six – landing

The horse will land with one foreleg leading. This will determine the leading leg of the canter stride away from the fence. As the hind legs meet the ground, the horse will stretch its neck forwards again to canter on.

Phase seven – get-away

The horse will push itself forward with its hocks well engaged. The get-away becomes more important as the horse begins to jump related fences. It should regain its balance and stride as quickly as possible, so that it will be ready for the next jump.

then reach the highest point of its jump too early, thus bringing down the back rails of the fence as it descends.

Bounce fences

These are very helpful in strengthening the horse. As an exercise they are very similar to humans doing push ups. They can be used as soon as the horse can cope with three or four fences confidently. As they are quite demanding, they should not be overused, particularly with young horses as they will tire quickly.

Placing poles.

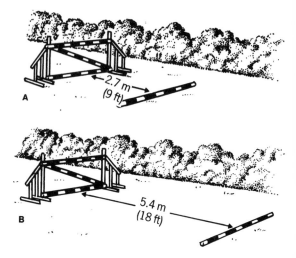

(a) Trot approach

(b) Canter approach with one
stride before the fence

TYPES OF FENCES

Cross pole upright

Cross poles encourage the horse to
jump straight through the middle of
its jumps and are useful for this
purpose at the beginning and end of a
line of fences. They can help to
encourage a horse to pick up its
forelegs, particularly if the fences are
quite high.

Straight bar upright

Upright fences should be used to
practise getting the correct stride for
the approach and take off. Because
there is no back rail, the horse will
not lose too much confidence if it
gets it wrong.

Parallels

These are used to encourage the horse
to stretch over the top of the fence.
They can be either an ascending
parallel, which encourages the horse
to fold its forelegs and reach the

Bounce fences.

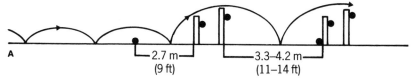

(a) Canter approach

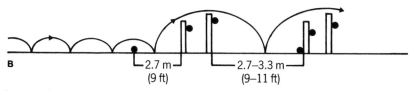

(b) Trot approach

The head and neck give the first impression.

The horse's senses are well developed.

Above left: The Thoroughbred is built for speed and stamina.

Below left: The warm blood is strong and powerful.

A horse in good health.

Above right: A young horse working correctly on the flat.

Below right: A horse with a good walk will form a V with the foreleg and hind leg on the same side.

Dressage horse and rider.

Right: Dressage training develops obedience and harmony.

Introducing the young horse to poles.

Above: **First work over a single pole.**

Above right: **Then two poles, 2.7 m (9 ft) apart.**

Below right: **When the horse is confident, put the third pole in the middle.**

Above left: Horse and rider show jumping.

Below left: Jump the young horse over small obstacles to increase its confidence.

Below: Correct training helps to develop a good technique.

Horse and rider across country.

Left: The event horse must be brave.

A well-turned-out show horse.

Right: The thrill of the chase is tremendous.

A hunter clipped and plaited.

A cross pole upright.

A straight bar upright.

An ascending parallel.

A true parallel.

highest point over the top of the fence, or the more difficult, true parallel. Jumping parallels helps to develop the horse's athletic ability.

Other fences tend to be a variation on similar themes to those mentioned. However, the horse should be introduced to all the more common types of fences, such as walls, gates and fences with fillers.

PROBLEMS

Running out

Why is the horse running out? Has it been overfaced? Did you catch it in the mouth last time over the jump? Is this a strange new jump that has taken it by surprise? Has the horse seen fillers, a wall, a ditch before? Is there something worrying in its line of vision over the fence?

The horse must learn to jump everything first time but in order to do this it must have confidence in you and believe that you will not ask too much of it nor allow it to be hurt or frightened. If the distances are right, the jump is properly built and not too high nor frighteningly new and strange, then the horse should jump it. Running out can quickly become a bad habit and is most unseating for the rider. If you think the horse has been overfaced in some way, go back a stage to jump something that the horse has no problem with and then progress gradually to the new jump. If it is just naughtiness, you must present the horse again and use your whip. The horse must learn to come in straight and go first time.

Stopping

Take the same course of action as for running out. The rider must ride positively and not drop the horse in front of the jump nor look down into the base of the jump. Many jumping problems are caused by rider error.

Rushing

Rushing is a serious problem because it makes the horse jump long and flat which means that it will tend to bring down higher jumps or could even tip up over cross country jumps. Often a horse that is rushing has its head so high in the air that it cannot see the jumps as it approaches them. This is very dangerous and can cause a bad fall.

Rushing may be caused by pain or fear. If you think the horse is in pain, have its back and legs checked. If it is caused by fear, then go back to less challenging jumps in the training and try to rebuild the horse's confidence. If the rushing is caused by sheer excitement, try circling in front of the jumps until the horse settles and do your ordinary schooling work in an area containing jumps until the horse accepts them as everyday things that it does not need to get wound up about. When you do jump, come in on a short approach in trot or even in walk to a low jump. If the problem persists, seek expert help in reschooling the horse.

JUMPING COURSES

When the horse is confident over grids of fences, progress to jumping small courses. If possible, practise these at home and make the turns for the approach easy and the fences inviting. For most people, unfortunately, the only chance they get to jump a course of fences is at a competition. Most shows run classes for novice horses, but it is important to check that the course has been built by someone knowledgeable, as poor turns, incorrect distances and uninviting fences will soon put both horse and rider off. The British Show Jumping Association (BSJA) runs special classes for young horses, both affiliated and unaffiliated, and they are well worth going to. Another important consideration is the ground that the course has been built on. If it is uneven or hard, it will affect the way the horse jumps. When riding a course, key points to rremember are:

U Ride the horse in a consistent rhythm between fences.

U Be prepared to rebalance or activate the horse in between fences. Don't leave it until you are approaching the fence.

U Unless you are against the clock, use as much room as possible to make your turns into the fences. Make sure that your turn brings you into the middle of the fence.

U Relax and enjoy it!

COMPETING

Walking the course

It is important to walk the course so that you can check the distances between fences and work out where to turn for the best approach to a fence. As you compete more, you will also find out the types of fences that you have to sharpen the horse up for and ride more strongly at. Also, check where the start and finish lines are, as you *must* pass through both or you will be eliminated.

Tack and equipment

Most shows adopt the rules of competition set by the BSJA, so their rules regarding tack and equipment will apply.

The horse

The rules regarding saddlery are not as strict for show jumping as they are for dressage. However, the following are *not* allowed in the arena:

U Running reins or any rein acting through sheaves or pulleys.

U Blinkers.

U Horses may not wear a Market Harborough, hackamore or any other form of bitless bridle.

The rider

The following are compulsory:

U Riding hat of specification BS 4472 or 6473.

U A shirt with a stock or tie (usually white).

U A riding jacket.

U White, pale yellow or fawn coloured breeches.

U Whips must be between 45 and 75 cm (17½–29½ in).

Jumping distances for ponies and novice horses

Between fences 1.2 m (4 ft) high:
One stride: 5.95–6.55 m (19½–21½ ft)
Two strides: 8.55–9.75 m (28–32 ft) (9.45 m (31 ft) if second jump is a spread)

Warming up
During the warm up, you should aim to loosen the horse and get it thinking forward if necessary, so that it is very responsive to the leg, and also build up its confidence by jumping practice fences. The practice fence should start at a modest height and then build up to the height in the ring. Don't overjump your horse as you will tire it unnecessarily.

Jumping studs
These are essential as they will give the horse security and confidence. If the horse feels that the grip is not good underfoot, it will hesitate when jumping. Different types of stud can be used depending on the going.

CHAPTER 7

FITNESS AND TRAINING FOR EVENTING

An event horse requires the obedience of a dressage horse, the agility of a show jumper and the heart of a warrior. It is the lack of this last quality that makes some horses totally unsuitable for eventing. Even if they are sufficiently talented, if they are not bold and brave they are not up to the job. Eventing was first used by the army to test the fitness and agility of both horse and rider. Today's sport has developed a highly efficient system of competitions that develop and test the horse up to high levels of endurance; probably the most famous being the three-day event held yearly at Badminton. The British have long been one of the nations at the forefront of eventing as the British tradition of hunting has produced horses and riders that are brave, bold and fast across country. Today's sport is so competitive that the horse has to be good in all three disciplines, although its ability across country is still the most important factor.

PREPARING FOR COMPETITION

The event horse should follow the

same basic training patterns as described in Chapters 5 and 6. The dressage phase tests the horse's obedience and correct basic training, the show jumping tests its obedience, agility and correct jumping technique and the cross country phase puts all these to the test, plus the horse and rider's courage. Once the horse has become reasonably balanced and obedient and has developed the necessary basic strength and jumping technique over fences, then it is ready to start cross country schooling.

Like show jumping training, the main aim of cross country schooling is to develop the horse's confidence and introduce it to the various hazards that it will meet in competition. It is best to start by jumping small versions of these, probably 61–76 cm (2–2½ ft) in height. This is important as it will enable you to urge the horse on if it does stop and look at the fence. Once a horse realises that it can stop if it doesn't like the look of a fence, then it becomes unreliable and possibly even dangerous when riding across country. However, if you overface the horse and frighten it with big fences, it will become equally unreliable. Often, inexperienced riders try to build their own confidence by charging their inexperienced horses at big fences. This is usually a recipe for disaster. It is most important to develop the horse's confidence and technique first over show jumps. After all, at the end of the day it is the horse that actually jumps the fence no matter how the rider feels about them!

PROBLEM FENCES

When schooling at home, you can build many of the different problem fences with jump poles. These will include bounces, corner fences, parallels and combinations. In Chapter 5, the importance of keeping the horse straight and to the middle of the fence was emphasised. This will pay dividends when you start training for cross country as you may need to jump fences at an angle and so the horse must be obedient enough to keep the line that you put it on and you must also learn how to ride a line. This is best practised first over show jumps.

Show jumps set up for jumping at angles.

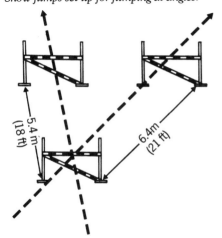

5.4 m
(18 ft)

6.4m
(21 ft)

The types of obstacles that must be practised at home are:

Water jumps
Water fences tend to cause many problems. Quite understandably, the horse is wary of jumping into water as, naturally, it does not know that it will be no deeper than 30 cm (1 ft). As far as the horse is concerned, it could be a bottomless well! Water fences become even more of a problem when they get churned up and the water becomes cloudy, as then the horse cannot see the bottom. The best way to introduce a horse to water is to find some still water, perhaps a shallow pond, and ride into it following an experienced horse. Let the horse stand in the middle of it and then walk in and out. Next progress to trotting through it until the horse seems confident. It is essential that the water fence has a nice, easy slope into it, so that the horse is not asked to jump until it is confident. The next stage is to progress to jumping up a small bank out and then over a small drop into the water.

Banks and drop fences
These tend to frighten riders more than horses. The horse must be taught the technique of jumping up and down small banks and drops until it is quite happy to do so in trot and canter. Larger banks and drops should not then prove too much of a problem, although they will require more impulsion.

Ditches
Ditches tend to worry both riders and horses. Start by jumping narrow, shallow ditches and approach them

A well-designed water fence.

A well-designed bank complex.

A ditch fence.

with determination. You may find it easier to follow a more experienced horse in the early stages. All ditch fences must be ridden boldly. Ditches can be found in front, underneath, behind and even between fences, so it is essential that both you and the horse gain enough confidence to jump them.

The other hazards that you will meet going across country are all variations on similar themes, so when the horse has gained confidence over show jumps and the type of fences described above, it will be ready to go to its first competition. This could be either a hunter trial, a Riding Club or Pony Club event or, if it has enough ability, a BHS Pre-Novice horse trials. Remember to select the first

few competitions with the following in mind:

U The fences should be solidly built and inviting.

U They should not be too high nor have difficult combinations. It is best to choose galloping courses to start with.

U At more difficult fences there must be an easy alternative, so that you can continue the course if you do have problems.

PREPARING FOR COMPETITION

The event horse has to be athletic and agile and have the stamina and endurance to cope with the cross

Dressage phase. The event horse should be calm and obedient.

country. This means that it will require a specific fitness training programme that will enable it to cope. After the general conditioning programme described in Chapter 4, the horse will have to spend about another six to eight weeks developing its strength and stamina. As with any fitness programme, you must first look at what the requirements are for that type of competition so that you can include in your programme the type of work that will be needed.

REQUIREMENTS FOR A BHS NOVICE ONE-DAY EVENT

○ **Dressage** The horse must perform a test at BHS Novice level. The training for this will be as described in Chapter 5. However, the event horse will have developed more stamina and endurance than the dressage horse, so it may become more excitable and tense in its work. Dressage schooling must be included all the way through the programme from week six until the competition. The horse will need to be schooled at least two to three times a week to remain supple and obedient.

○ **Show Jumping** The horse must jump a course of fences between 1.10 m (3 ft 7 in) and 1.15 m (3 ft 9 in) in height with spreads of up to 1.20 m (3 ft 11 in) at the highest point. The course must include at least one double. The horse should be jumped from week six onwards. It will probably do more work over show jumps than cross country fences – remembering that you can build the fences to ask the same questions. The horse should be jumped at least twice a week, and this may include some show jumping competitions.

○ **Cross country** The course will be between 1600 and 2800 m (1750–3058 yd) in length. It may be over different types of terrain, steep hills, undulating or flat land, so the horse must be worked over them all. The horse must canter at a speed of 520 m per minute (568 yd) to enable you to get home within the optimum time. If you are over this time you will receive penalty points. Judging canter speed takes experience, so in the early days it is a good idea to mark out a stretch 250 m long in a field and time how long it takes to canter this distance. If you are at the correct speed you should pass the second marker in just under 30 seconds.

It is essential that the horse is capable of cantering the distance at the required speed before it competes. The course will have between eighteen and 28 fences with a maximum height of 1.08 m (3½ ft) and a spread of 1.2 m (3 ft 11 in) at the highest point. Drop fences must not exceed 1.68 m (5½ ft) and ditches are between 2.74 and 3.05 m wide (9–10 ft).

The horse must have completed the basic training before starting the fitness programme, so it should only need to school over cross country fences a few times before the competition. The most important thing is to establish the horse's ability to work at the required speed over different terrain including hills.

TRAINING FOR SPEED AND ENDURANCE

The work done in the first six weeks will have conditioned the body and developed some fitness. This can now be built upon by introducing canter work. The trot work should be continued and possibly made a little

The cross country phase. The cross country tests the boldness of horse and rider.

Left: Show jumping phase. Show jumping tests the horse's technique.

more demanding. Hill work is essential to develop stamina; it is also essential that the horse learns to balance itself going up and down hills in trot and canter. If incorrectly ridden, horses tend to hollow and shorten their stride when going up and down hills and this would make it very difficult to jump if required. The horse must be taught to work to the bit in a correct, active and balanced way. Steady canter work should be done daily, for about four to five minutes, from week six. The canter should be done first on the flat and then inclines should be introduced over the next few weeks. The canter speed can be increased as the programme progresses and by the last two weeks you will probably be able to canter for up to two six-minute

sessions daily, one of which can be at the speed required for competition. The horse must be active in its canter, so if it is lazy you may need to get after it!

It is senseless to overtrain the horse, as undue stress could be damaging. Look at what the competition requires and plan accordingly. It is also important to monitor how the horse reacts to the work. If it tires easily, then a longer, steadier programme may be needed. If it appears to be getting a bit above itself, include more dressage and jumping schooling instead of some of the canter work. All programmes vary as people have different ideas but, basically, the programme must put progressively more stress on the body so that it can adapt accordingly

A horse working down a hill correctly.

and will cope with the requirements of the competition. This means at least an eight–twelve-week programme, which must include some small competitions to build confidence in both of you. Go to small hunter trials and try also to do schooling rounds at cross country courses that are open for this. Local show jumping events will be fun and will help to settle both your nerves.

Interval training

It is appropriate at this stage to mention interval training. This system of training has been adapted from a system used to train the human athlete. Basically, it works on the principle of inducing intervals of controlled stress on the body, allowing time to recover partially and then stressing the body again. As the programme progresses, the body will recover more quickly and allow harder work. To be done correctly, the horse's temperature, heart and respiration rate must be monitored before, during and after work. This requires someone on the ground to help you and the experience and knowledge to know when everything is normal. It can be a useful system of training, but it should not be undertaken without experienced help and for one-day eventing, it is not really necessary. As emphasised earlier, you must be aware of how the horse reacts to its work as this will tell you if it is fatigued. Although you may feel you need to ask a little more, a tired horse may damage itself, so be sensible and if in doubt don't push it.

COMPETING

As one-day events combine the three disciplines of dressage, show jumping and cross country, they require more preparation and equipment than other types of competition and this is explained in Chapter 9. You will be given starting times for the three phases. Arrive in plenty of time, report your arrival at the secretary's tent and collect your number.

Walking the course

The cross country course can be walked the night before. It is best to walk the course at least twice to familiarise yourself with the route, terrain and lines of approach that you wish to take. It is a good idea to walk the course with someone experienced so that you can discuss how to ride the different fences. The following points should be thought about:

U Check the flagging of each fence. The red flag should be on your right as you jump the fence and the white on your left. There may be different routes at more complicated fences, so check carefully.

U At more difficult fences there will be easier alternatives. Have an emergency plan in mind in case you have a stop or the horse is not going as well as it might over the course. You must be careful that you do not cross your own path in front of a fence as this will result in penalty marks.

U At combinations or fences that can be jumped at angles, the course builder will often have given you a landmark in the distance – such as a tree – to aim at for the best line. Check and see; if not, try to choose one anyway.

U Make a note of the going and also look out for course indicators that guide you when you are in the open.

U At competitions where there is more than one level of class, there will be some fences that are not to be jumped by you. These will be indicated by coloured markers. Jumping the wrong fence will result in elimination.

The show jump course should also be walked as soon as possible as you will probably not get a chance during the day.

Crossing your own track.

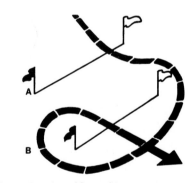

Crossed tracks – 20 penalties

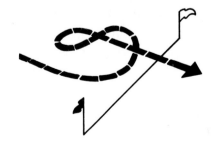

Presented and then crossed tracks – 20 penalties

Working in

Working in for the dressage and show jumping phases has already been covered in Chapters 5 and 6, respectively. There will be plenty of time in between sections for you to cool the horse off and make it comfortable. Before going cross country, many people will take out the horse's plaits, as they like to have some mane to grab hold of in an emergency!

Working in for the cross country must achieve the following aims:

U The horse's heart rate is gradually increased to that of galloping speed, which can be as high as 200 beats per minute. This is done by working the horse for two to three minutes in walk, then two to three minutes in trot and then the same at a steady canter. This will also loosen the horse and get its circulation moving and its respiration rate up.

U The horse must be responsive and alert to the leg and rein aids. This can be done by riding transitions.

U The horse must be jumped over a couple of fences to find its stride and gain confidence. You will have show jumped already, but it is advisable to jump the practice fence to make sure the horse is responsive.

Riding the course

You should be warming up at the start at least fifteen minutes before you are due to go. The starter will call you to the box and count you down to start. Set off at a nice steady rhythm with the view to increasing the speed as you feel confident. Keep the horse in balance and be prepared to steady it in between fences if it starts to get too strong. Remember your planned route and stick to it; only change if things are not going too well, when you should follow your alternative plan. Don't be tempted to make sudden rash decisions as you approach a fence as it could put the horse wrong and cause trouble.

You should check the response of your horse as you go round. If it feels tired, then finish the course gently. Often horses are overenthusiastic over the first half and will tire themselves out if you are not careful. When you have passed the finish, slow down gradually to help to bring the horse's heart and respiration rates down more gently. At a safe distance from the finish, dismount, loosen the horse's girths and lead it back to the box.

After–care

When you reach the box, remove your tack and, if the horse is not blowing too hard, offer it a small drink of water. Quickly check it over for injury. Some people like to use some form of cooling agent on their horse's legs to stop any swelling. This should be applied as soon as possible. The horse may be allowed to graze and should be washed down if the weather is not too cold. The horse should be grazed and walked in hand for at least twenty minutes before being dressed to travel and loaded in the lorry. This will allow it time to cool off. It should be offered short drinks (about half a bucket) at twenty-minute intervals until it is no longer thirsty.

TACK AND EQUIPMENT

The tack and equipment allowed for dressage and show jumping are the same as described in Chapters 5 and 6. However, you are *not* allowed to work in using any gadget, such as bearing, running or balancing reins. The horse *is* allowed to wear a figure of eight noseband for the dressage. For the cross country, the horse may have any type of bridle, but may only wear a running or Irish martingale. Protection for the horse's legs is a matter of preference. If exercise bandages are used, they must be well secured either by stitching the bandage or with adhesive tape. Whatever protection is used, it *must* be made secure for reasons of safety.

An exercise bandage.

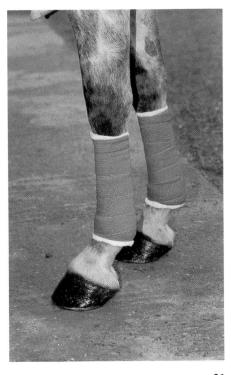

Studs

These are essential for the jumping phases, and most people will use them for the dressage as well, as this is usually on a grass arena.

Rider's dress

At Novice level, the rules for rider's dress for the dressage and show jump sections are the same as described in Chapters 5 and 6. For the cross country section, the rider must wear a body protector, preferably one of the makes recommended by the Jockey Club. A crash helmet of BS 4472 and a hunting stock are recommended; the latter will support the neck in the event of a fall. Most riders will choose colours to be identified in when going cross country. There are no restrictions to this as regards tops or silks but breeches must be either white or buff in colour.

CHAPTER 8

FITNESS AND TRAINING FOR HUNTING

The tradition of hunting in Great Britain spans many centuries. Although horses are now used in many different sports, hunting still employs many people, both directly, as grooms in stables, and indirectly, as farriers and saddlers. In modern times, hunting has an uncertain future due to pressure from groups that are against what they consider to be a cruel sport. However you may feel about hunting, it has established many of the traditions and standards that have been adopted in the horse industry worldwide, one example of this being the British staff who are much sought after for their high standards of stable management.

As a horse, the hunter is bred to be bold and fast across country, and yet have the conformation to make it a balanced and comfortable ride. This has meant that this type of horse has also been much sought after by competition yards.

PREPARING FOR HUNTING

The previous chapters have dealt with the correct training of the competition horse. Much of what is required there is also desirable in the good hunter. It must be well schooled and obedient, balanced and willing. It must have a good jump and be fit enough to stand up to the rigours of a day's hunting. A suitable fitness and training programme probably most resembles the one used for the Novice event horse.

There are different types of hunting: fox hunting, stag hunting and hare hunting (harriers), to name but a few. These have different seasons, but for the purpose of this book we shall look at the requirements for fox hunting.

FOX HUNTING

Traditionally, the season starts on the first Saturday in November and will run until the farming activities in that particular area stop it, i.e. lambing or crop planting. Before the season proper starts, there is cub hunting. This does not involve the hunt in chasing fox cubs, it is so called because it is when the young hounds are trained to work as a pack. As a member of a hunt, it is considered correct etiquette for you to cub hunt when possible as you will thus help the hunt on horseback. When the actual hunting season starts, many people view this simply as a chance to charge across other people's land. Certainly, the thrill of the chase is tremendous but it is important to remember that the hunt does have a serious job to do, namely to control the population of foxes, which farmers consider to be vermin.

The hunter should follow the same basic conditioning process as described in Chapter 4 and will then continue on a similar programme for speed and endurance as described in Chapter 7. Hunting does not have its exact requirements written down as in eventing, but the hunter must be capable of galloping for up to 3–5 km (2–3 miles) and trotting for about 16–19 km (10–12 miles) while hunting. Some days it may do more; other days less. The amount of jumping done out hunting all depends on the rider and the type of country. The old-fashioned prints showing horses jumping big hedges in open country are typical of only small areas of Britain now. However, the horse must be capable of jumping what it is asked to in good style. Hunter trials held in early autumn are intended specifically to encourage this.

PREPARING FOR THE MEET

To hunt for a full day, your horse needs to be stabled so that it can be clipped out and kept fit. It is possible to do some hunting from the field, although you will not be able to follow for long or go at any speed. It is important to remember that the careful conditioning and fitness programmes that have been described in previous chapters are necessary to ensure that the horse copes with the work with minimal risk of injury or to its health. If you have not been working the horse, you must not overexert it as this could result in physical distress.

After the opening meet, it is correct to plait the horse when hunting. If the horse is unclipped, then you can go without plaiting, although you should then wear a tweed jacket, not a black or navy coat. Meets are usually at 10.45 a.m., so unless you have far to travel, you can stick to your normal feeding routine, although it is important to remember that the horse should be fed at least three hours before fast work to let the stomach clear. The stomach's close proximity to the diaphragm makes it uncomfortable for the horse if fed too soon before fast work.

If the meet is very local, you may hack to it. This is better for the horse as it allows it to settle and loosen up before standing around at the meet. If you do box, then you should stop about 3 km (2 miles) away from the meet's venue for the same reason. Many people travel their horses in full tack. This is fine for short distances as long as you allow plenty of room, otherwise the saddle can get damaged on the partitions.

CARE OF THE HORSE WHILE HUNTING

During the day you should do your best to ensure that your horse is comfortable and prevent it from

Good manners

Hunting has traditions of etiquette, and the following points are important to remember:

U Say 'Good morning' to the Master, hunt staff and officials.

U Always stay behind the Field Master and follow his instructions.

U When hounds are passing, turn your horse so that its head is facing them and its quarters are away from them. This also applies when the huntsmen's horses are passing.

U If possible, carry a proper hunting whip, with a long lash, so that you can trail it around the horse if hounds get too close. This is the best way to prevent them getting underneath the horse or around its legs.

U If your horse is young and not experienced out hunting, tie a small green ribbon in its tail to warn other riders. If it is liable to kick, then use a small red ribbon.

U When crossing land, be courteous to the landowner and stick to the edge of the field. *Never* gallop across crops or a field with stock in it.

U If you are the last through a gate, ensure that it is shut.

U When jumping, look out for others.

U If fencing is damaged by the hunt, notify the Field Master. It is the hunt's responsibility to repair it.

U At the end of the day, say 'Good night' to the Master.

injuring itself. The following points should be observed.

U Do not go at speed unless it is necessary.

U Try to trot off the road when possible.

U When standing around at a covert (a clump of bushes or trees), walk the horse if the weather is cold or the horse is hot and blowing.

U Don't be tempted to go on when you feel the horse has had enough; there is always another day!

U Walk the horse the last couple of miles to the box.

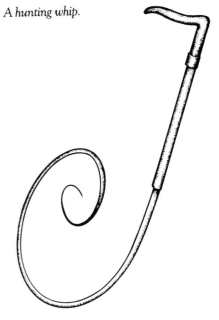

A *hunting whip.*

A hunter breast plate.

U When you have dismounted, loosen the girth but leave the saddle on for about ten to fifteen minutes to allow the blood to return to the area gradually. If it rushes back too fast, it could rupture a blood vessel and cause a sore.

U Put on light rugs to travel the horse, so that it does not get too hot.

U Check for any obvious signs of injury.

CARE ON ARRIVAL HOME

U Remove all tack and allow the horse to roll.

U Offer a drink of water. If a horse is hot, it is best to take the chill off the water by adding some hot water. This prevents stomach cramp.

U Check the horse over for injury. If its legs are already wet, then hose them down. Rinse its tail in a bucket of water anyway, to remove the worst of the mud.

U Make sure the horse has plenty of hay to eat. Some people give a bran mash but this is only advisable if bran is usually fed daily. If it is not, such a sudden change in diet could destroy the bacteria in the hind gut. It is much better to give hay and later a small concentrate feed.

U Rug the horse up with light rugs and take out its plaits. Some people put stable bandages on the horse's legs to prevent filling.

U Leave the horse in peace for a while and go and rinse the worst of the mud off the tack.

U Check the horse later. If it is dry, re-rug it for the night. If you have not already done so, give it a small feed. Make sure it has plenty of water.

TACK AND EQUIPMENT

There are no specific guidelines for tack. Traditionally, people used to hunt in a double bridle. These days, anything that the horse is happy in can be used. It is best to have a jumping saddle, as you will need to ride shorter. It is advisable to put a breast plate on the horse, particularly if the country is hilly. Boots can be put on the horse for protection, although you may find that they will rub if they are on for long periods.

Rider
There are more specific guidelines for the rider. Only the Master and huntsmen wear scarlet jackets. Followers wear hunt coats that are black for men and either black or navy for women, with a white or cream stock. If you are cub hunting or the horse is not clipped and plaited, then you should wear a tweed jacket. Breeches should be cream, although gentlemen who wear brown-topped hunting boots should wear white breeches. Hats are a matter of preference. Traditionally, people used to wear bowlers and sometimes top hats at lawn meets. Hunt caps are still worn although many people now sensibly wear the new safety hats, BS 4472 or 6473.

CHAPTER 9

TRAVELLING AND CARE AT COMPETITIONS

The competition horse will travel extensively to national competitions. Top level competition horses will also travel internationally, by air or ship. Correct care of the horse while travelling is essential as it can greatly affect its performance. A horse that sweats excessively will lose vital body salts (electrolytes) and will be deficient in these later when the body requires them during fast work. If the horse suffers a bad journey, it can be unsettled or, worse, injured. The travelling of horses internationally requires great care and is often left to specialist companies. Most horse owners will travel their horse within Britain either by lorry or trailer.

PREPARING TO TRAVEL

Checking the vehicle
This should be done regularly. If you are towing with a car, then you should have both vehicles checked and serviced. After three years old the car has to pass an MOT every year, so it should not be in too bad a condition. If you have a lorry, it also has to pass an inspection by the

Ministry of Transport but unless it is used regularly, it should be started and checked at least monthly.

Trailers can be more of a problem. They do not have to have any form of official inspection to check that they are safe and roadworthy, so often things can go undetected until they become dangerous. The following checklist should be used regularly for all vehicles.

- ᔕ The vehicle has the necessary tax, insurance and documentation to make it legal to drive on the roads.

- ᔕ The engine has sufficient oil and water.

- ᔕ There is enough fuel.

- ᔕ All tyres have sufficient air (this can vary when carrying loads) and the tyres have enough tread and are not perished.

- ᔕ The electrics, for lights etc., work.

- ᔕ The floor is sound. Most floors are wooden. They can be checked for rot by pushing a knife into the wood. This should not be possible if the wood is sound.

U Check that the brakes work. This is essential if the vehicle has been standing around for a while, as brakes can seize up.

The horse

The horse should have adequate protection, even for a short journey.

U **Headcollar and poll guard**: Ideally, these should be leather in case the horse pulls back as nylon webbing can cut and burn the horse. It is advisable to put a poll

guard or some form of padding over the top of the headcollar. Blows to the poll can be fatal and many trailers and lorries tend to have rather low ceilings.

U **Leg protection**: There are many different types of travel boot on the market. Whichever type you use, they must provide good protection especially to the coronets, the heels, the knees and the hocks. If well designed, they are good to use as they are very quick and easy to put on and take off. Alternatively, you can

A headcollar with poll guard fitted.

Equipment

It is essential to make a list of everything that you will need to take with you and tick it off as you pack it. What you take can vary depending on the type of competition and the length of time that you will be away. The following checklist includes essential items that should be taken whenever you are competing.

U Water and buckets. It is best to have your own supply of water as sometimes at shows it can be contaminated. On a long trip, it may be necessary to give the horse water during the journey.

U Feed and hay. It is important to try to stick to the normal feeding pattern as much as possible. However, when eventing, feed should be withheld for three hours before the cross country, due to the close proximity of the stomach to the diaphragm.

U Bedding for the horse. This is essential if you are staying away, along with mucking out tools.

U Simple first aid kits, both human and equine.

U Documentation. This must include the horse's vaccination certificate, and ideally your confirmation of entry.

U A change of rugs. The horse may break out and require lighter rugs.

U Grooming kit.

U Studs and a small spanner or key. You should have a selection of different studs.

A travel bandage.

use stable bandages with extra padding underneath them. Knee boots should be used to protect the knees, along with over-reach boots to protect the heels, and hock boots.

U **Rugs**: It is advisable to use some form of rug to protect the horse from any protruding edges on the partitions. If it is very hot, however, it will be uncomfortable for the horse to wear a rug. Horses often sweat up when travelling, so do not over-rug it and take along lighter rugs to put on in case the horse gets too hot.

U **Tail protection**: The horse must have protection on its tail. Horses often lean on their hind quarters for balance, and the tail can be rubbed sore if not protected. A tail bandage and tail guard are best, although you can use two tail bandages, one on top of the other. It is also a good idea to plait the tail or put it in a stocking to prevent it from getting soiled during the journey.

LOADING

When loading the horse, it is important to remember to make everything as inviting as possible. Horses will be reluctant to enter a low, dark trailer, so, if possible, buy one that has good head room and a front ramp that can be opened when loading. Many horses will also be reluctant to enter a narrow space, so move the partition over. Position the box so that it is alongside a wall, to prevent the horse going to one side, and also position it so that the horse is loading towards the yard as it may

be reluctant if it is going away from its friends. Always allow plenty of time to load unless you know the horse will be good. If the horse is difficult, it is important to assess the situation. Is the box inviting? Is the horse genuinely scared or is it just being naughty? Many horses only need a slap on the hind quarters, or lunge lines crossed behind their hind quarters, whereas others require gentle coaxing.

THE JOURNEY

Remember that the horse will be using its strength to balance itself and that this can make travelling stressful. Drive carefully and try not to brake sharply or take corners too fast. If you are on a journey of over three hours, you should plan to stop and water the horse and possibly feed it.

Dressed for travelling.

If the horse is difficult to load, lunge lines can be crossed behind its hind quarters.

CARE OF THE HORSE WHILE COMPETING

Correct care of the horse at the competition is important to ensure good performance and health, but it is equally important that the horse is correctly cared for before and after the competition. Good stable management is essential for the horse's good health and well being but, for the purpose of this book, we shall look at the care of the horse the day before, the day of, and the day after, the competition.

The day before

The trailer or horse box should be checked as described earlier in this chapter. It is important to remember to put fuel in the vehicle, particularly if you have an early start, as many petrol stations will be closed.

The horse should be exercised as normal. If you are travelling that day, then only give it light exercise, as travelling is tiring for it anyway. You may wish to bath the horse before the competition but this should only be done if the weather is not cold. It is better to wash the horse a couple of days before the competition so that some of the oils can return to its coat and encourage it to lie flat. The mane is very difficult to plait when it has just been washed, so do that a week before. Check the horse's shoes, and, if it has studs, clean out the holes and replug them with cotton wool. This will save time and temper at the event!

Feed as usual. There is no point in feeding extra concentrates the day before a competition as it takes two to three days for the feed to be fully digested. If the horse's training requires more energy, then gradually increase its feed during the training programme. If the horse is eventing, some people advise cutting down on hay rations a couple of days before the competition. This will ensure that the horse is not carrying too much bulk in its intestines.

TACK AND EQUIPMENT

Tack should be regularly taken apart, cleaned and checked thoroughly for safety. Particular attention should be paid to the condition of the leather; there should be no cracking or splitting. All stitching must be secure. The following checklist should be made for safety:

U The leather of the girth straps and stirrup leathers must have no splits or cracks, particularly around the holes.

U The stitching must be secure. Particular areas are where the girth straps attach to the tree of the saddle, the buckles on the girth and stirrup leathers, and all stitching around the buckles and straps of the bridle.

Deciding what tack to take will be governed by the official regulations laid down in the rule book and the tack that the horse works best in. If you are eventing, it is advisable to take a spare girth, a spare pair of reins and extra stirrup leathers.

There are also rules dictating the rider's dress. These should be checked and the right clothes packed. Again, it is a good idea to make a list and check things off when packed.

AT THE COMPETITION

For dressage and eventing, you will be given starting times. If the competition is far away, it may be necessary to travel the day before. It is always better to allow plenty of time to prepare and plait the horse for the competition and have enough time when you arrive to let the horse settle and for you to get your bearings and perhaps have a cup of coffee! If you are both calm, then you will perform much better. If you are eventing, it is essential that you take somebody with you. If you were unfortunate enough to have a fall, you might need someone to drive the box home.

Working in
This has already been discussed in previous chapters. However, it is important to remember that the horse will rarely perform as well at competitions as it does at home. Do not be impatient; you will learn by experience how much or how little working-in time you need to prepare the horse.

Feed and water
Water should be offered at regular intervals during the day, particularly if it is hot. Loss of fluid from sweating can cause the horse to dehydrate. This leads to further problems, including loss of performance. If the horse is doing fast work, it should be walked until it stops blowing before being offered water or feed. The normal feeding routine should be stuck to as closely as possible, although you must take into account

the following:

- ∪ Feed at least one and a half hours before working. This allows the stomach to clear.

- ∪ Withhold feed for at least three hours before fast work. This ensures that the stomach is clear. The stomach lies just behind the diaphragm. If it is full it will make breathing uncomfortable.

Grooming
The horse should be kept comfortable by being groomed in between classes. If it is a hot day, you are better to wash the horse down with water. This will cool it and wash the sweat away, preventing the tack from rubbing. If you wash it thoroughly, the horse should be grazed or walked in hand until it is dry. Check the horse over thoroughly after each class for any cuts or heat in the legs. Remove the plaits when the horse has finished the classes that require it to be plaited. If you damp the mane down well, you will be able to wash out the curls.

Tack and equipment
It is a good idea to clean as much of the equipment as possible when it has been finished with. This will save you time when you get home.

THE JOURNEY HOME
The horse will be tired after the competition and the journey home will tire it further. Proper after care is essential for the horse's well being. It should be unloaded and walked for ten minutes or so to allow it to loosen up. Tie it up in the stable and remove all its travel equipment, remembering to check for any injury. Let the horse loose to roll and then rug it with light rugs. Offer water and then give a hay net and a small feed.

The vehicle should be unloaded and the box mucked out. It is advisable to lift the bedding and allow the floor to dry. Check the horse an hour later and come back later again to change its rugs if necessary.

The day after
The horse should be thoroughly checked over again for any injury or heat in its legs or feet. Then it should be walked out and trotted in hand to check that it is sound. If it normally goes out in the field, it should be turned out for a couple of hours to allow it to loosen its muscles. Otherwise, it should be lightly worked.

All tack and equipment should be cleaned and prepared for the next competition.

INDEX

Page numbers in *italic* refer to the illustrations